THE OECD MODEL CONVENTION – 1996 AND BEYOND

Income of Professional Partnerships
Employees as Permanent Establishments

50th IFA Congress
Geneva 1996

THE OECD MODEL CONVENTION – 1996 AND BEYOND

Income of Professional Partnerships Employees as Permanent Establishments

Proceedings of a Seminar held in Geneva in 1996 during the 50th Congress of the International Fiscal Association

Vol. 21c

Chair: Klaus Vogel (Germany)

INTERNATIONAL FISCAL ASSOCIATION

KLUWER LAW INTERNATIONAL
THE HAGUE — LONDON — BOSTON

Kluwer Law International
P.O. Box 85889
2508 CN The Hague
The Netherlands

Library of Congress Cataloguing-in-Publication Data

The OECD model convention, 1996 and beyond : proceedings of a seminar held in Geneva in 1996 during the 50th Congress of the International Fiscal Association / edited by International Fiscal Association.

p. cm. -- (IFA congress seminar series : v. 21c)
ISBN 9041110291 (hb : acid-free paper)
1. Double taxation--Congresses. 2. Tax administration and procedure--International cooperation--Congresses. I. International Fiscal Association. Congress (50th : 1996 : Geneva, Switzerland) II. Series: IFA congress seminar series : no. 21c.
K4474.6 1996
341.4'844--dc21 98–21733

ISBN 90 411 10291

THE OECD MODEL CONVENTION – 1996 AND BEYOND

Income of Professional Partnerships Employees as Permanent Establishments

Proceedings of a Seminar held in Geneva, Switzerland in 1996 during the 50th Congress of the International Fiscal Association*

Chair of the Seminar:
Professor Dr.iur. Klaus Vogel (Germany)
University of Munich (Emeritus)

Panelists:
Daniel Lüthi (Switzerland)
Vice Director of the Swiss Federal Tax Administration; Chairman Fiscal Affairs Division, OECD

David Oliver (United Kingdom)
Partner, Coopers & Lybrand, London

Jacques Sasseville (Canada)
Principal Administrator, Fiscal Affairs Division, OECD

Professor Arvid Skaar (Norway)
Norwegian School of Management, Sandvika

Philippe Thiria (France)
Head of Tax Department, Unilever, Paris

Michael Waters (United Kingdom)
International Division, Inland Revenue, London

Secretary:
Dr. Irene Salvi (Switzerland)
Schweizerische Rückversicherungsgesellschaft, Zürich

* *The views expressed are those of the authors and not necessarily those of the International Fiscal Association*

IFA CONGRESS SEMINAR SERIES*

1. Work in Intergovernmental Organizations on Transnational Companies (Congress 1976) (out of print)
2. The Revised OECD Model Double Taxation Convention on Income and Capital (Congress 1977) (out of print)
3. Fiscal Policy and Tax Structures in the Pacific Region (Congress 1978) (out of print)
4. UN Draft Model Taxation Convention (Congress 1979) (out of print)
5. Recourse to Tax Havens – Use and Abuse (Congress 1980) (out of print)
6. Taxation of the Income Arising from the International Seabed (Congress 1981)
7. Imputation Systems – Objectives and Consequences (Congress 1982)

* Available from Kluwer Law International
(*for Europe and Rest of World:*)
Order Department,
Kluwer Law International
Distribution Centre, PO Box 322,
3300 AH Dordrecht, The Netherlands.
Tel.: +31 78 6546 454
Fax: +31 78 6546 474
Toll free: 0800 963 955 (UK customers only)
email: sales@kli.wkap.nl

(*for USA, Canada, South and Central America:*)
Order Department,
Kluwer Law International
675 Massachusetts Avenue
Cambridge, MA 02139, USA
Tel.: (1–617) 354 0140
Fax: (1–617) 354 8595
Toll free in USA: (800) 577 8118
email: sales@kluwerlaw.com

8. Tax Policy towards the National Heritage (Congress 1983)

9. Adjustments for Tax Purposes in Highly Inflationary Economies (Congress 1984)

10. International Tax Problems of Charities and other Private Institutions with similar Tax Treatment (Congress 1985)

11a. Taxation of domestic shareholders on undistributed income of foreign corporate affiliates: objectives, technique and consequences (Congress 1986)

11b. International Tax Treatment of Common Law Trusts (Congress 1986)

12. Taxation and Human Rights (Congress 1987)

13a. Data Processing in Taxation (Congress 1988)

13b. Tax Consequences of Pension Provision for the Internationally Transferred Employee (Congress 1988)

Draft EC directives on parent-subsidiary, on mergers and on arbitration (Congress 1988) (out of print)

14a. International Taxation of Services (Congress 1989)

14b. Tax Treaties and Domestic Legislation (Congress 1989)

15. Double Taxation Treaties between Industrialized and Developing Countries; OECD and UN Models, a Comparison (Congress 1990)

16. Tax Treaties and Local Taxes (Congress 1991)

17a. Advance Ruling: Practice and Legality (Congress 1992)

18a. Harmonization of Corporate Taxes in the EC (Congress 1993)

18b. The Taxation of Employee Fringe Benefits (Congress 1993)

18c. Corporate Tax on Distribution (Equalization Tax) (Congress 1993)

18d. Environmental Taxes and Charges (Congress 1993)

18e. Resolution of Tax Treaty Conflicts by Arbitration (Congress 1993)

19a. International Taxation of Dividends Reconsidered in Light of Corporate Tax Integration (Congress 1994)

19b. Secondary Adjustments and Related Aspects of Transfer Pricing Corrections (Congress 1994)

19c. How Domestic Anti-Avoidance Rules Affect Double Taxation Conventions (Congress 1994)

20a. Dividend Access Shares (stapled stock) (Congress 1995)

20d. Taxation of Non-Resident Entertainers

21a. Taxation Issues in a Federal State and Economic Groupings with Concurrent Taxing Authorities (Congress 1996)

21b. The Influence of Corporate Law and Accounting Principles in Determining Taxable Income (Congress 1996)

21c. OECD Model Treaty – 1996 and Beyond (Congress 1996)

21d. Visions of the Tax Systems of the XXI Century (Congress 1996)

22a. OECD Model Convention – 1997 and Beyond (Congress 1997)

22b. Cross Border Valuation for Income Tax, VAT and Customs Duties (Transfer Pricing) (Congress 1997)

22c. Taxation of Expatriates (Congress 1997)

22d. Presumptive Income Taxation (Congress 1997)

TABLE OF CONTENTS

Introductory Notes
Klaus Vogel 1

Work of the OECD – I
Jeffrey Owens 3

- The communication revolution 3
- The globalization of financial markets 4
- Trade, investment and tax issues 7
- Transfer pricing 8

Work of the OECD – II
Daniel Lüthi 9

Allocation of Profits under Article 14 11

- Introduction: the persons covered by Article 14 11
- Differences between fixed base and permanent establishment 13
- Attribution of income: the first example – the writer 14
- The deduction of expenses for the purposes of Article 14 17
- The second example – the architect 18
- The third example – the law firm 23
- The fourth example – the law firm assigning a partner to another country 25

To What Extent Do Employees Assigned to a Subsidiary Constitute a Permanent Establishment of the Parent Company? 29

- The *Alphawell* case – the right to use facilities 32
- The length or frequency of use 34
- Agency permanent establishment 35
- Comments from the audience 41
- Concluding remarks 43

Appendix 1: Outline on Article 14 45
Appendix 2: Outline on Employees as a Permanent Establishment 55
Appendix 3: The Origins of OECD Model Articles 7, 14 and 15 67

Introductory Notes

Klaus Vogel

The seminar on development and selected topics of the OECD Model Tax Convention organized jointly by OECD and IFA has become an appreciated regular feature of IFA Congresses. The present publication renders account of the papers delivered and the discussions held in the context of this seminar at IFA's Congress in Geneva in September 1996. OECD was represented at the panel of the seminar by Mr. Daniel Lüthi, Vice Director of the Swiss Tax Service and Chairman of OECD's Fiscal Affairs Division; Mr. Jacques Sasseville, Principal Administrator at that Division, and Mr. Michael Waters of the United Kingdom's Internal Revenue. Speakers nominated by IFA were Mr. David Oliver, partner in the London Office of Coopers & Lybrand, Visiting Professor in International Taxation at the London School of Economics and co-editor of the *British Tax Review*, United Kingdom; Professor Arvid Skaar from the Norwegian School of Management in Sandvika, Norway, and Mr. Philippe Thiria, Head of the Tax Department, Unilever, France. Secretary to the seminar was Mrs. Irene Salvi from Switzerland.

The first and foremost part of the seminar was constituted as usual by reports delivered by Mr. Owens and Mr. Lüthi on current and upcoming work of the Committee on Fiscal Affairs and in particular, its Working Party No. 1 which is in charge of the Model Convention. For the subsequent panel discussion two subjects regarding interpretation of that Convention had been selected, one under its Article 14, the other under its Article 7. An informal note on the origins of Articles 7, 14 and 15 is reproduced in Appendix 3.

Regarding Article 14 the emergence of big international professional partnerships like accounting and law firms with partners in several countries has given rise to new problems, in particular how and to whom income derived by such partnership is to be allocated. Article 14 assigns taxation in a way similar to Article 7, but the wording of both articles differs to some extent. It is unclear, therefore, whether a partner of a transparent professional partnership is taxable with a share of the partnership income wherever the partnership has a fixed base, comparable to the partner of a transparent business partnership having permanent establishments in other countries, or whether as the wording of Article 14 may suggest he is taxable only to the extent to which the fixed base 'is available to him ... for the purpose of performing his activities'. Moreover, Article 14, in contrast to Article 7, has no rules on how to determine the income attributable to a fixed base.

With respect of Article 7 the panel discussed to what extent employees delegated to a subsidiary constitute a permanent establishment for the parent corporation. This may not be of high relevance for the corporation as long as the employee is engaged in supervising the subsidiary or giving technical or commercial advice, for in such cases his activity would not produce any significant income. It may, however, be important for the taxation of the employee himself, who if his activities constitute a permanent establishment might become taxable under Article 15(2)(c) of the Model Convention.

Both topics elicited a lively discussion as may be seen from the following.

Klaus Vogel
Chairman of the Seminar

Work of the OECD – I

Jeffrey Owens

As usual, it is always a pleasure for us to come to these IFA conferences. We are particularly pleased with the continuation of these joint seminars. For us it represents a way of getting input from the business community into our work and already in fact we can see how helpful that is from the discussions that we had at the last conference at Cannes, so we look forward to the continuation of this initiative.

What I would like to do is to take ten minutes briefly to outline some of the emerging issues that are preoccupying our Committee on Fiscal Affairs. You should have received at the entrance a little brochure called Fiscal Affairs, and that provides a relatively comprehensive description of the activities that we are currently undertaking, so I do not need to go over all of those activities. What I would like to do, though, is perhaps identify three areas which I think will be taking up an increasing part of our time over the coming years. Those three areas are, first, the tax policy implications of the communication revolution, secondly, the tax policy implications of the globalization of financial markets and the third area is the interface between investment, trade and tax. I would just like to say a few words about each of those areas and then I will mention transfer pricing, as I know that some of you are quite interested in where we stand in our work in that area.

The communication revolution

First then the communication revolution. We are concerned about what are going to be the implications of the development of what has come to be called the information super highway. This is not just the Internet; it is the development of smart cards, it is the development of new communication technologies.

Part of the implication, I think, of these new technologies is that there is a breakdown of national boundaries and a weakening of the linkage between the place where the services are performed and the place where they are consumed. Now these new technologies will require us to look at a number of issues. I shall just identify two. The first would be what are the implications for some of the concepts that are built into our tax systems. Under the income tax for example, under double taxation treaties, can we continue to use the concept of effective management, are we going to have to review the concept of permanent establishment, can we continue to stretch that concept to encompass these new activities, or in fact do we have to consider thinking the unthinkable that we may have to replace the concept itself, so there are a whole set of issues there I think on income tax that we would be looking at. Similarly under the value added tax questions arise: how do you adapt the concept of place of supply to activities that are carried out through the Internet, how do you adapt that to the development of electronic commerce?

So those are some of what I call the substantive tax principles that are embedded in our tax systems that we would need to review because of these technological developments. That in a sense is the negative side perhaps of these developments, but I think there is also a positive side in that these technologies open up new possibilities for tax authorities in terms of the way that they assess and the way that they collect taxes. So we would be looking at both of those aspects.

This work in fact started almost a year ago, primarily on the VAT. In two weeks time we will have a discussion in Dr. Lüthi's Working Party (Working Party No. 1) on the tax treaty implications and this will then lead into a discussion at the January 1997 meeting of the Committee on all of the broad issues that arise here, but also on the dangers that are posed for tax authorities by these developments and the new opportunities that they open up. I was very pleased to see when I was coming in here that the Permanent Scientific Committee has endorsed a project in this area and we at the OECD look very much forward to working with IFA on this topic.

The globalization of financial markets

The second set of issues are very much related to the whole question of the liberalization of financial markets. When I looked through our work programme, and we have four working parties of three special sections and I have forgotten how many working groups we have at the moment – it is a lot. But if there is one theme that runs through all of that work, it is always linked to developments in financial markets.

I would just like to pick out three areas which I think are going to preoccupy us over the coming years. The first is what could be called the spread of tax competition for financial and other services. In a sense, I think what happens with globalization is that it increases the pressure on countries to design special tax regimes to attract these types of activities – activities which are, by their very nature, geographically very mobile. I think what we are concerned about here is not just the way in which traditional tax havens operate, because that is something that we have come to live with, although looking at the use of tax havens would be part of this work, but also the way in which what can be referred to as normal tax countries, European countries, countries that you find in North America, in Latin America, in the Asian region – these countries are increasingly being pressurized to put in place special regimes to attract particular types of activities – headquarter regimes, coordination regimes, offshore financial centres.

We are concerned that if there is not some action taken in these areas, then there is a great danger that the tax base will be undermined – the tax base as it applies to income and capital. So in this sense, there are some quite serious revenue implications from these developments.

The second reason why we are concerned about these developments is that they have the potential to distort the international allocation of capital between countries. So those are the reasons which led us to launch this project last June. It is a project which has strong political backing. You may have noticed that in the communiqué that was issued at the last OECD ministerial meeting, there were in fact three sentences on this issue. It does not sound much, but believe me, getting three sentences into a ministerial communiqué at the OECD is a major achievement and you certainly will have noticed that when the heads of the G7 countries met in Lyons in July, they devoted a whole paragraph to this issue, so there is strong political backing to do something and I think the two questions that we will be addressing are: 'Can we distinguish between what could be seen as acceptable forms of tax competition and what could be seen as unacceptable forms of tax competition?' And if we can make that distinction, I believe then we obviously go on and ask the second question: 'What do we do about harmful forms of tax competition? What can be done at the national level, what can be done in the context of tax treaties, what can be done at the international level?' So that is a project which I think will take up a lot of our time. We have to report back to the ministers by Spring 1998, so I hope that we meet that rather ambitious timetable.

The second area where I think there are major implications of the globalization of financial markets is in the way we have seen the development of new financial instruments and new financial techniques, global trading for example. These developments clearly pose major challenges for tax authorities. Again can we apply some of the traditional concepts, does the development of new financial instruments undermine some of these concepts, for example the distinction between debt and equity – is that workable any longer – perhaps not. Clearly we will need to see if we can continue to apply some of these concepts, at what are the alternatives? We hope to have a report that will look at some of the issues that arise in this area towards Spring of next year. That report will be accompanied by a separate report which will deal with the issue of global trading, because we feel in fact that this is an issue which deserves separate treatment. It is also an issue which is quite closely related to the work we are doing on transfer pricing. The global trading paper will probably come out around February/March of next year.[1]

The third implication of the globalization of financial markets is the way that countries tax cross-border interest flows. My impression is that at present anybody who pays tax on cross-border interest flows is either extremely honest or extremely badly advised and that effectively means that most cross-border interest flows are tax free. The question is: 'Can we continue with that situation?'

There are three alternatives that governments face. One – accept this and say 'Fine, we shall now just change our duty practices, change our national legislation and just accept that these types of income flows are not going to be taxed'. There may be some attractions in that. In a sense it takes us one step nearer consumption tax. There may be administrative attractions in that it simplifies the administrative work of the tax authorities, but there are also dangers. It reinforces the tax bias in favour of debt financing, for example, and also it raises the question that if you do not tax cross-border interest flows, can you continue to tax interest flows purely at the domestic level? But that is one option.

The second option is to say that maybe the way to deal with this is to put in place a general withholding tax; that is an option which is still on the agenda of the European Community. I think there will be a number of issues that will have to be dealt with if one wanted to pursue that. First of all, and most importantly, one would have to decide on how you define interest. That in itself has become a major challenge, precisely because of the development of these new financial instruments, and you would also have to build up political support for this. It would require that some major OECD countries reverse their policy of not taxing interest that is paid to non-residents.

The third alternative is to look at whether we can improve exchange of information (and here I am not talking about putting in place new legal provisions – I am talking about the practical operation of exchange of information provisions) and the key question there is: 'Can tax authorities get better access to banking information?' This raises the question of bank secrecy. So all three

1. Now released as a discussion document.

of those options have advantages and have disadvantages. I would not try, at this stage, to anticipate what the outcome will be – but I think this is clearly going to be an area of debate both within the OECD and within the Community over the coming years. We would hope that we would have some results available towards the end of next year.

Trade, investment and tax issues

Let me now turn to the last and third theme that I believe will occupy us quite a lot over the coming years and this is the linkage between trade, investment and tax issues. In the past, there has been a tendency to put these three issues in separate boxes; you have a box labelled 'trade', a box labelled 'investment' and a box labelled 'tax'. The conceptual framework which you used for each box was different, the way that the rules were administered was different and the civil servants that were responsible for each box were different and rarely talked to each other. I think that what is happening, again partly in response to globalization, is that there has been a breaking down of these barriers and increasingly we are seeing that tax comes into the discussion on trade, that tax comes into the discussion on investment and, when you think about it, that is not surprising.

Most non-tax barriers to trade and investment have been removed as a result of the work done on GATT. So what are you left with – taxation. So I expect to see that this mixing of trade, tax and investment issues will come to the forefront of the debate we have at the OECD. Let me give you two examples of that.

We are currently working on what we call a multilateral agreement on investment and this is intended to be a state of the art agreement which would materialize the extensive network of bilateral investment agreements. One of the key issues at this work is whether or not it should cover taxes. At one extreme one can say that we have got the double taxation treaty network, therefore the main investment issues that arise in the tax field are already dealt with and therefore we can carve out taxes from the agreement. At the other extreme, one could argue that there are gaps, even between countries that have extensive tax treaty networks, and of course you have the problem of countries that do not have such networks. And there are some major players that do not; Chile, for example. So, if you accept that, you would want the agreement to cover taxation. At this point, my feeling is that there will be an extensive carve-out for taxation but there may be some tax provisions that we find in the agreement. We have to finalize that work by Spring of next year.

A second example of this interlink between trade, investment and tax is the work that we are doing on the tax treatment of bribes of public officials. You may have noticed that we came out with a recommendation last Spring that recommended to countries that they should review their treatment of bribes, particularly the question of whether or not bribes to foreign officials are deductible. Part of the reason for that recommendation was the feeling that the current practices are distorting competition, so you get the trade aspect coming in. Part of the feeling was also that the tax system in certain countries was actually condoning what, I think everybody would agree, is a practice that one would not want to encourage, namely, bribing of public officials.

Transfer pricing

Let me conclude by just saying briefly where we stand on the work on transfer pricing. We issued the chapters on intangibles and services and I am sure you have seen these at the OECD publication stand. We expect that the next chapter to be issued will be that on cost contributions. Hopefully, that could come out in the Spring of next year. With the issuing of that chapter, I feel that we will have concluded the core part of the guidelines. We shall then move on and look at the application of the guidelines to particular activities, primarily in the financial area. So we will look at the application of the guidelines to global trading. We will look at the application of the guidelines to the concept of permanent establishments, especially in the banking sector and to the insurance sector as well. So that I think brings you up to date on where we stand.

Work of the OECD – II

Daniel Lüthi

I must say that Working Party No. 1 much welcomes the opportunity to have these common meetings and I most appreciate your presence here, not least because all of you had to get up quite early this morning and that I am not the only one to sit here. Working Party No. 1 deals with a number of issues and amongst them are issues that were brought up by the private sector. As a start, I will give you a survey of the current structure of Working Party No. 1. Since a number of years, a so-called steering group prepares the work of the Working Party in relation to the revision of the Model Convention. It may propose to the Working Party changes or additions to the Model or the Commentaries. It may also submit the issue to the Working Party without proposing any solution, or propose to establish a Working Group to deal with a highly technical issue. For the time being the Working Party has four Working Groups. Working Group No. 1 examines the application of the OECD Model Tax Convention to partnerships, trusts and other non-corporate entities. In the past, the work on this issue did not gain any conclusive results; the Working Party hopes that this time it will be more successful. Working Group No. 2 deals with the taxation of cross-border pension payments. Working Group No. 4 discusses a number of issues related to permanent establishments. Finally, Working Group No. 5 examines issues that arise in relation to Article 14 (Independent personal services). These Working Groups are not of a permanent nature. Depending on the needs, new Working Groups may be established and existing ones abolished.

Working Party No. 1 will meet at the end of this month in Paris. It will have to deal with a number of important issues.

On the issue of Article 14 the main question will be whether the Article shall be kept or be deleted and amalgamated with Article 7. Then a first interim report on permanent establishments will be discussed in which a number of issues are brought up by the Working Group. The Working Party will also start work on the impact of the communication revolution. There will also be a meeting with selected non-member countries. This is an important activity which allows the OECD to explain to non-member countries what the OECD is doing in order to give them a better understanding of the preferred solutions of member countries. Together with the next update of the Model a supplement will show the position of these countries with respect to the Model provisions. Besides this, the Working Party will have to deal with the next update to the Model Convention. The September 1996 condensed version of the Model includes the 1995 update. There will be no 1996 update but we expect to have enough material for the 1997 update.

With respect to Article 12 (Royalties) the next update will contain a clarification of the beneficial ownership requirement. Besides, it is probable that changes to the Commentary concerning software payments will be made.

The update will also contain some drafting changes in the English version of the Model which have been made for the purpose of gender.

The update may also contain clarifications in the Commentary on the meaning in Article 15 of the term 'employer', on what is meant by remuneration 'borne by' a permanent establishment and on benefits in kind covered by the Article.

Another issue to be dealt with relates to goods or services attributable to a permanent establishment especially in the case of a building site or construction or installation project. A clarification in the Commentary may be helpful in order to avoid that some kind of a force of attraction principle is applied.

The term 'place of effective management', is not defined in the Model Convention and the Commentary does not provide any indication as to its meaning. The Working Party will have to decide on an addition to the Commentary on Article 4.

Another issue arises under paragraph 2 of Article 17 (Artistes and sportsmen). When a non-resident artiste or sportsman is employed by a sham company resident in a third State, the question has to be answered whether the Model Convention or domestic law applies.

The Steering Group of the Working Party is dealing with a number of issues concerning the Model Convention. The catalogue of issues contains, for the time being, about 100 active issues. This does not mean that the issues are active and that the working party is passive but we already dealt with a number of issues. There are many more in the catalogue and so for the time being we have around 100 but you realize that with these short meetings twice a year – we cannot do everything at the same time. We have to set priorities in this area. At its next meeting the Steering Group will deal with a number of matters on income related to international air transport, withholding taxes on dividends and on interest, the legal status of the Commentary, the taxation of capital gains, on shares in real estate companies, dividends paid by non-resident companies, problems that have arisen with Article 19 (Government service), drafting improvements to Articles 4 (Resident), 6 (Income from immovable property), 7 (Business profits) and 8 (Shipping and air transport), the need for a source rule for royalties, the comparison of a permanent establishment with local entities in the light of non-discrimination, and the revision of Article 2 (Taxes covered).

Allocation of Profits under Article 14

Introduction: the persons covered by Article 14

David Oliver:
You all will have a copy of the outline[1] which tells you something of what we are going to discuss and in particular in the outline you will find copies of the slides which we will be projecting on the screen.[2] The way we propose to present this subject is to say maybe first a few words in separate sections on three aspects of Article 14 and then to proceed to the examples because it is in discussing the examples that we can then bring out some of the points we wish to raise.

The first aspect that we wanted to touch upon by way of a start, and starting from a very simple position, is: 'Who are the persons who are covered?' And the particular question is 'Does it include companies?' because if it does not include companies then that is of course an important difference between Article 14 and Article 7.

Article 14 simply refers to a resident of a contracting State. That is then defined in Article 4(1) as any person who under the law of that State is liable to tax, etc. The term 'person' includes an individual, a company and any other body of persons, we are told by Article 3(i)(a). So at that point I think one would conclude that if one was looking at the definition of a resident of a contracting State one would say, yes indeed, it did include a company.

There are three points to be made in showing that this is not entirely a certain conclusion. First of all in the latest Model, Mexico actually adds an observation to the Commentary. It says that Mexico considers that this Article is applicable to companies that perform professional services. Why would Mexico take the trouble to say that it applies to companies that perform professional services if everybody thought that it did include companies?

The second point that comes up is with a US reservation to the effect that the US originally considered that Article 14 did not extend to companies and entered

1. Appendix 1.
2. These illustrations are included in Appendix 1.

a reservation. The US has now withdrawn that reservation, so that would suggest that the US thinks it does not apply to companies. Indeed, of course, in the US model they do not apply Article 14 to companies, but we are looking at the OECD Model.

So there are two straws, or indicators, there that suggest the term does not include companies. But clearly if you are looking at the definition of resident of a contracting State, then a company is in that definition. And I think the point that it then raises, my third point, is whether there is something in the definition of professional services which means that the services you are looking at in Article 14 are not the sort of services that could be provided by a company, and apart from the question whether or not a company is within the definition of a resident of a contracting State, whether the services you are looking at are services that could only be provided by individuals or individuals in partnership. That was as far as I wanted to go by way of introduction on that point.

Michael Waters:
Now the working group at the OECD which is looking at Article 14 naturally took this as one of the first matters it considered and virtually every member of the working group said that in practice they applied Article 14 only to individuals and did not apply it to companies. There was one exception: Turkey will apply Article 14 to legal entities although Turkey has not entered an observation or reservation to say so, unlike Mexico. I understand that, in practice, Canada also applies Article 14 to legal entities and again they have not joined with Mexico in their observation because there is nothing in the Commentary which says that Article 14 applies to individuals. So why Mexico felt it necessary to make an observation on the point which is not covered in the Commentary has always struck me as quite odd. I think in practice, historically, the sort of activities that come within Article 14 have been performed only by individuals. It has not been common for members of liberal professions to incorporate. But this is now becoming more common and there is certainly a question about whether it should remain valid that Article 14 should apply only to individuals. There is also the question of partnerships. If a partnership is transparent, then most OECD countries would agree that each individual partner comes within Article 14. But if the partnership is not transparent, if the partnership is taxed as a legal entity, we have the same question as we do with a company: should the non-transparent partnership be within Article 14? There is one further point arising out of this which I think we shall come to when we look at the second example, which has to do with the scope for an individual to pick and choose whether he or she comes within Article 14 or Article 7 by choosing to incorporate. If it is true that Article 14 applies only to individuals, then an individual

may be able to escape from Article 14 into Article 7 simply by forming a company for the purpose of a particular contract. Now there is a policy question about whether that is desirable. But we shall come back to that later.

Differences between fixed base and permanent establishment

David Oliver:
May I say that in everything that we discuss from now onwards in relationship to partnerships, we are always going to be looking at a transparent partnership. We are going to be assuming throughout the discussion that the partnership is transparent and, though we recognize that there may be issues with hybrid entities which are treated as a transparent partnership in one jurisdiction and as a company in another, as Mr. Waters has just mentioned, we are not actually going to be discussing those bodies.

Let us go on now to the fixed base and there were some comments in the outline about possible differences between the fixed base and the permanent establishment. I would just like to draw attention to perhaps three points here. The first of course is that different words are used and if you use the expression 'fixed base' in one place and the term 'permanent establishment' in another place, you presumably mean something different or otherwise you would not have chosen different words. The Commentary itself says in paragraph 4 that it was thought that the concept of permanent establishment should be reserved for commercial and industrial activities: the term 'fixed base' has therefore been used. One of the thoughts in looking at possible differences and how important they may be now is that this wording goes back a long way and there was an element in the Model of a distinction between the businessman who is in commerce, who is buying and selling things and makes a profit, and the professional man, who renders fees to his clients and derives an income. It is almost, I suggest, like a matter of social status. The professional man is found in Article 14 and the businessman is found in Article 7 and Article 5.[3]

The question now is whether, with developments such as have been mentioned a few moments ago where professional activities may well themselves be undertaken by companies, this is any longer a relevant distinction to have. So the first point is that different words have been used – 'fixed base' against 'permanent establishment' – and that seems to be deliberate as it says in the Commentary. The next point is that in Article 5 we have paragraphs 3 to 7. Now I accept

3. *See* Appendix 3 for a discussion on the origins of Articles 7, 14 and 15.

that paragraph 7 about parent companies would not necessarily have a relevance in Article 14 if it was not applying to companies. But there is a question as to what extent do paragraphs 3 to 6, at least, of Article 5 become incorporated into Article 14. If 'fixed base' includes these agency arrangements on terms as set out in Article 5 – then why does it not say so in Article 14? Why does Article 5 go to this trouble to spell out the agency rules and Article 14 does not? So does this suggest that a fixed base is slightly different? I think that the only example, though the members of the audience may think of other examples, where the point was considered was in a US Revenue ruling that is noted in the outline,[4] where the US fisc looked at the position of a French concert performer who was appearing on a tour in the US and was represented by an independent agent. The way they analysed it, was to say that fixed base is not defined in the treaty. When we look back at the definition of permanent establishment which is somewhat similar, and if we apply these agency rules, we find that this is an independent agent and therefore the concert performer does not have a fixed base. So those are a couple of points on fixed base.

Attribution of income: the first example – the writer

Let us go on to look at our first example. This first example is the purest case which you can think of under Article 14. And the reason for presenting it is that it acts as a benchmark, if you like, as a contrast to other cases that we shall be looking at later on. Here in this case we have a writer and a publisher and we have four countries involved. We have chosen quite fictional names for the countries so that you will not be distracted by thinking about whether the wine in this country is good or the climate in that country is particularly pleasant, although you will presumably be able to derive some information on that from the movements of the writer. The writer enters into a contract with the publisher. The publisher is in Utopia. Under that contract the writer receives an advance payment. Now that is a sort of non-returnable advance, it is income to the writer, it is a first instalment of payment for the book. It does not matter whether the manuscript is completed or not, that is income to the writer and let us not worry about whether the writer is going to receive royalties later on: there is some income received by the writer. So the writer begins work: she then moves to Arcadia and spends the Summer there writing. The writer then returns to Ruritania. However, for the purposes of this novel, certain research is required

4. *See* Appendix 1.

in Illyria and so we find that the writer goes to Illyria for the purposes of this research. She stays there for two months, moving around and staying in various small hotels or private houses. The writer then returns to Ruritania where she then completes the manuscript. Now the issue which is raised by this example is: 'Where is there a fixed base?' and because it overlaps, 'What is the income which is attributable to the different activities?' Perhaps, Chairman, having introduced the example in this way, I might turn to Professor Skaar who has some comments that he would like to make on this.

Arvid Skaar:
The issue I would like to address at this point is whether or not there are differences between the fixed place of business that would apply to normal business activities and the fixed base that applies to the writer here and to the liberal professionals we have here in the later examples. And the short answer to the question is yes, there are probably some differences, although they may not be intended from the OECD's point of view, but they may have been developed in practice, in the course of time. The fixed place of business, in the notion of permanent establishment, consists of three conditions. First of all, you need to have a place of business – and anything can be a place of business if it is a substantial and a physical object which can be used as a base for a business activity. So it excludes intangibles and it excludes portable equipment. In this case, I would say that it was not a big problem because this person would need somewhere to work. So she has a place of business for this purpose. And normally the liberal professions would have that and I do not see any specific authority for the conclusion that the two concepts here are different. So that would be the same condition.

Then, the second condition is that this place of business should be located at one specific place. That has been interpreted so that it should be located all the time at this one specific place. But practice seems to accept that the place of business has been moved around, if it still remains in one place for a specific period of time. Normally in these cases here, in liberal professions, that would not be a problem because these writers or architects in later examples will have an office, or something like that, which is located in one specific place. Then the third condition will raise some differences and that is the permanency or the duration of the activity. It seems in practice, although I think that there is no written legal authority, that tax authorities have required shorter times for liberal professions compared to normal business activities. I have seen cases where one month has been considered enough for a liberal professional whereas six months would normally be required under the permanent establishment. So that is one difference that should be noted. It could be different in different countries but it is possible that the time required is shorter. And then the second point is that it seems that permanent establishment is more sensitive to interruption in the business activity than the fixed places. It seems that it would be more easily accepted that the taxpayer moves in and out for a period of time. It is part of his business to be a little bit here and a little bit there. Whereas, under the permanent establishment, it seems that it is required that the taxpayer should carry on his business on a regular basis and not be interrupted too much. He does not have to be in the country all the time but it should be carried on, on a regular basis. Those two differences are something that should be looked at, I think. Otherwise, it seems that the conditions are more or less the same between the fixed place of business and the fixed base. This conclusion also has some authority in the Commentary which says that the same principles should also apply.

Michael Waters:
This example raises the question of the relationship between Article 14 and Article 12, because this writer receives an advance payment. An advance payment may be perceived to be an advance payment of royalties and certainly the author might receive royalties and there is no rule in Article 14 explicitly dealing with the conflict that is resolved for Article 7 by the paragraph at the end which says that other special articles will take priority. The second issue is a very practical one. Speaking as a tax inspector in Arcadia or Illyria, the chances are that I will never know this writer has been here. But I have a warning for a certain American author who came to the UK two years ago and was signing copies of her books. She mentioned in a presentation she gave that the previous year she had spent six months in the UK carrying out some research. I now realize I made a mistake. I asked her to sign a copy of her book. I should also have asked her to sign a tax return. Perhaps a member of the US delegation could make himself or herself known, afterwards, and I will post a copy of this tax return form for the writer. The final issue concerns in fact the question of research. If a writer comes for, say, nine months to conduct research, a period of nine months is a nice long time and may well give rise to a fixed base. But what if the writer only comes for one month to do research? That is a very short period of time. And this raises the question of whether one can use the suggestion in the Commentary on Article 5 about permanent establishments. The Commentary says that if the place of business was not set up merely for a temporary purpose it can constitute a permanent establishment, even though it existed in practice only for a very short period of time because of the special nature of the activity of the enterprise. So if a research project is very narrow and can easily be dealt within one month, it is arguable that this can be a fixed base, even though it was of short duration, because the short duration was all that was required to carry

out the activity in the country concerned. One can only say that it depends on all the facts and circumstances, but I am more than ever convinced that the American writer owes me some tax for her research activities in about, I think, 1993.

The deduction of expenses for the purposes of Article 14

David Oliver:
Let us move on now from this example and come to another one in a moment, although we may refer back to this example in discussing the attribution of income under Article 14. Let me say a few further words about the relationship between Article 14 and Article 7. I mentioned earlier that Article 14 deals with income whereas Article 7 deals with profits. This gives rise to the question as to what extent you can deduct expenses in computing income for the purposes of Article 14.

One view would be that Article 14 effectively incorporates all the provisions of Article 7. But, as with the fixed base in Article 14 and the questions of agency, Article 14 simply refers to the income attributable to the activity and the provisions in Article 7, in particular Article 7(2) treating the permanent establishment as a distinct and separate enterprise, are not actually referred to in the text itself in Article 14. Indeed you might wonder how, in relation to the writer, you would treat the writer as a distinct and separate enterprise dealing at arm's length with herself. That in itself may be a good reason for not putting such wording into Article 14. That also may be a reason for saying that Article 14 does not apply to companies, because you can split up a company and you cannot split up an individual. The Commentary on Article 14 seems to believe, though I think there is an ambivalence there, that the provisions of Article 7 are incorporated in Article 14. It says in paragraph 3: 'the provisions of the Article are similar to those for business profits and rest in fact on the same principles as those of Article 7. The provisions of Article 7 and the Commentary thereon could therefore be used as guidance for interpreting and applying Article 14'. If that is so, why not include those provisions in the text? Why were they not included in the text? Then there is a curious point for native English speakers: in the following paragraph, paragraph 4 it says that 'even if Article 14 and 7 are based on the same principles, it was thought that the concept of permanent establishment should be reserved for commercial and industrial activities.' Now this is where maybe the English in the OECD Model does not bear too much analysis by an English speaker. Because, in English, the use of the words 'even if' suggests disapproval or disagreement with something. The little boy is sitting at lunchtime with a plate of food in front of him and a glass of milk. And the father says to him: 'Eat up your lunch'. And he says 'No, I will not'. And the father says: 'Even if you do not eat the food that is on your plate, you should drink the glass of milk'. In the English usage, there is a sort of disagreement there with the son's decision. So when the Commentary says *even if* Article 14 & 7 are based on the same principle, on that construction it suggests that the Commentary is not really approving of that interpretation. I do not want to make any more of that; I think it may simply be a drafting point. However, it is an issue as we shall see in the example that we come to now, which is the architect.

The second example – the architect

In this example we have an architect who practises in Ruritania and he has two clients in Utopia. Those two clients each have projects lasting over a three-year period and they are located quite close to one another and he therefore rents an office in Utopia and uses that as a drawing office, as a base, for his visits to Utopia. And let us say that these may take place every 3–4 weeks and each visit lasts for 3–4 days. Now though the whole of the fee income from the Utopian projects is derived from the Utopian clients, some part of it is attributable to the activities in Ruritania. There is an interesting point here which other panellists may wish to comment on, in that it is the income which is attributable to the activities. It is not necessarily to the work performed. What would happen if the architect went to Utopia on one of his visits, finds that he needs some additional information or data for the purpose of that visit, returns to Ruritania to collect it, and comes back again and continues his work? Now there is an argument, and I think one of the other panellists will comment on this, that the return visit to Ruritania is actually attributable to the work he was doing in Utopia. So it is not actually the sort of place of performance of the services, it is the income attributable to the activity.[5]

Another point comes up if we change this example, because here we have assumed so far that we have a fixed base. Imagine now that the facts are rather different and the architect is not actually working for clients in Utopia but he is working for a contractor – his assignment is with a contractor who was building the project, and the contractor is a resident of some third country. Now the contractor then has a construction project in Utopia, but the construction project

5. More correctly, it is the income attributable to the fixed base – Sasseville's comments below on page 19.

falls within the provisions of Article 5(3). It does not last for more than 12 months. So what happens then? Well, if you were applying Article 5, in that case, you would say, and the Commentary covers the point, that planning and supervision is not included if carried out by another enterprise whose activities in connection with the construction concerned are restricted to planning and supervising the work. If that other enterprise has an office which it only uses for planning or supervision activities, relating to a site or project which does not constitute a permanent establishment, such office does not constitute a fixed place of business within the meaning of paragraph 1 because its existence does not have a certain degree of permanence. So if you took the view that Article 5 and the permanent establishment rules do indeed apply for determining a fixed base, you would say that our architect in that situation is covered by that rule. He does not have a fixed base. If you took the opposite view and said well actually, as I was saying earlier, Article 14 only refers to a fixed base and does not refer to the further provisions of Article 5 as to what in Article 5 may constitute a permanent establishment, then what would happen if the architect incorporated himself and he has a company, because then he has put himself into Article 5 and his company in Ruritania does not have a PE in Utopia? So, I think that there are one or two other comments the panel may have to make on this. In particular there is the point about the income attributable to the activities and this is the question of expenses as well.

Jacques Sasseville:
I will only focus on the allocation of the income between the fixed base and the other office. We assume here that there is a fixed base because that is what is stated in the example. Mr. Oliver has already identified the difficulty here between what the Commentary says and what the actual wording of Article 14 provides. This again is an issue which can be related to paragraph 2 of Article 3 – what is the meaning of the terms which are not defined in the Treaty? We have here in Article 14 a reference to income attributable to the fixed base and just to correct something that Mr. Oliver has said, it is not income attributable to the work performed, it is not even income attributable to the activities, it is income attributable to the fixed base. This is not defined in the Treaty, but does the context require you to go to Article 7? Otherwise, can you simply apply your domestic law rules whatever they are? So this is the issue that is raised. If we assume that the principle of Article 7(2) should be applied, as stated in the Commentary, then you have the concept of this separate independent enterprise. So you should attribute to the fixed base the income that the separate and independent enterprise would have realized. This raises all the issues that are discussed in the Commentary on Article 7 and in the report on Attribution of

Income to Permanent Establishments. So, in that particular case, let me present to you what the theory would be according to the principles that are stated in Article 7. I think in that case to split the fee income between the two States on the basis of the hours worked would not be the best method. Again, I am talking about the theory, if you look at what is recommended in the Commentary on Article 7, what we normally agree to be the fundamental rules applicable in such cases when you have a PE. You should basically look at the functions performed in a fixed base and the other office. So, if in that example, you assume that the function of obtaining the contract was performed when there was no office in Utopia, this is one function that goes to Ruritania. If you assume, as we did in the example, that the drawing and the research would be based in the fixed base, then these are functions to be attributed to the fixed base. So then what you do is, to consider what an independent enterprise would have charged for the drawing and the research. And then if you can find a comparable that is good, if not then cost plus would seem to be the type of method that would be applicable. What about those short return trips you have to make to Ruritania during your stay in Utopia? If those are for the purposes of the research, as stated in the example, and the research function has been attributed to the fixed base, it seems to me quite logical that the income relating to that would be attributable to the fixed base and the expenses of the return trip would likewise be attributed to the fixed base.

What about parts of the work that are performed in Ruritania? Then again you would have to identify what is that work. Is that related to the functions that are attributed to the fixed base, or are there other functions, for example, processing the data through a computer that could be allocated to the office in Ruritania because you do not have such facilities in Utopia? So I would certainly not say that no part of the income would be attributable to Ruritania because the contracts seem to relate to Utopia. I do not think that those are the principles that are stated in the OECD Model.

The only thing that I would like to say at the end is that this is the theory – what about the practice? And this is something you will be thinking throughout the morning. These guys are crazy – they are talking about the theory. We know, because professional services is our bread and butter, that practice is not like that. Well, at least in that respect the Commentary will support some practice here. If you go back to the Commentary on Article 7, in paragraph 24, there is a reference there to cases where other methods could be better. I am going to quote you a part from Article 24. 'Again in the case of a relatively small enterprise operating on both sides of the border between two countries, there may be no proper accounts for the permanent establishment, nor means of constructing them.' I do not know if the accountant of the architect, when preparing the tax return, will know about the principles that I have stated and whether he will be willing to engage in the research of the functions performed for that particular contract and maybe the other dozen contracts that have been performed in that context. It might not be the case – there might not be separate accounts. In that case, the Commentary says that you could determine the profits of the permanent establishment, and I would extend that to the fixed base, by reference to 'suitable criteria' and that means that I would not be too much upset by an allocation of the fee on the basis of the hours worked in each State. Again you have to be practical on issues like that.

Philippe Thiria:
As we have just seen, in order to determine what profits are to be allocated (the word 'profits' is in the title of the first subject of this seminar) two steps must be taken.

The first consists of allocating the fruit of the work performed and the profession carried out, which is what Mr. Sasseville has just looked at. The second relates to valuation: assuming there is a fixed base to which the benefits of a certain professional activity have been attributed, what profits should be taxed? This is where we come across one of the main differences in the wording of Article 14 and Article 7 of the Model Treaty. Article 14 merely refers to 'income' ('*revenus*' in French) without providing a definition. The word 'income' is therefore different from the word 'profits' in Article 7, and is defined nowhere.

The first comment which can be made is that, at least in French, the word 'income' is closely associated with the taxation of *individuals* and of *dependent* or *independent* activities.

In France, we have an '*impôt sur le revenu des personnes physiques*' (i.e. income tax on individuals) and an '*impôt sur les sociétés*' (i.e. corporation tax), although the latter is not a tax on the company's income. I do not know if this is the same in other countries.

The following question might then be raised: are we speaking of gross income which would be the equivalent of turnover for a business, or is it net income comparable to a result, a profit, or even a loss?

As Mr. Oliver put it so clearly, the text of Article 14 alone does not make it possible to answer this question. Indeed, unlike Article 7, in Article 14 there is no definition of 'income' nor method of calculating income.

Article 14 merely sets out the rule attributing the right to tax the income in question to one State.

However, as you can see from the documents provided to you, the Commentary of Article 14 refers back to the principles set out in Article 7. In particular, paragraph 3 of the Commentary of Article 14 refers to the 'allocation of profits', which is an indirect way of referring to Article 7 paragraph 2. And, as you know, this second paragraph provides for a kind of arm's length rule on the comparison with independent businesses.

Further, this same Commentary of paragraph 3 effectively deals with the question relating to the deduction of expenditure and explicitly refers to Article 7 paragraph 3.

The problem is that the Commentary does not bind the States. It is separate. Further, the text of Article 14 itself does not make it possible to establish a relation with Article 7.

I would like to point out that this issue which arises from the Model Treaty was resolved in a number of bilateral tax treaties: Article 14 is more specific and explicitly refers to the rules on establishing the taxable profits as stated in Article 7. This is notably the case of the recent Treaty signed between France and the USA.

But this explicit link is notably missing in the Model Treaty.

If we assume that the Commentary does not bind the States, the provisions of Article 7 do not apply; the States can then only apply the rule attributing the right to tax and the State in which the fixed base is established will be able to apply its domestic law independently and in full sovereignty. The taxable income can then be established easily, in accordance with the rules of internal law. This is clear and unquestionable.

However, what happens if the domestic law has different, less advantageous, rules for non-residents? This would be a clear case of *discrimination* as the non-resident with a fixed base in the State is less well treated than a resident of the same State carrying on the same business.

Can the taxpayer resort to Article 24 of the Model Treaty which deals with discrimination? Article 24, at least following my reading, does not appear to be of much assistance here. Indeed, the first paragraph deals with discrimination on the basis of nationality and this is clearly not the issue here. The following paragraphs do concern permanent establishments: they specify that the permanent establishment of a non-resident must not be taxed more heavily than a resident business carrying on the same activities at the same conditions. However, you are aware of the fact that this obligation is an obligation to actually achieve a result and not simply to take all necessary measures to ensure that the result is achieved. The tax burden must not be heavier for the non-resident whatever the method used to establish it. Unfortunately, like in Article 5, only the permanent establishment is referred to and not the fixed base. Resorting to Article 24 will therefore be of no use to the taxpayer.

Article 14 in its current state can therefore lead to a clear case of discrimination, for which there is no remedy, by imposing a heavier tax burden on non-residents than on residents.

The current text gives rise to a second kind of problem which would remain even if Articles 7 and 14 were directly related and the income referred to in Article 14 was indeed a net income.

The first difficulty arises from the fact that accounting rules and rules for calculating the basis of tax often differ according to whether they apply to professional activities or to commercial businesses.

The first difference relates to timing. Very often cash-in and cash-out movements are taken into account for the purposes of establishing the taxable basis for individuals, and not the accrued receivables, debts which are certain in their principle and provisions for future losses and expenses, which are taken into account in relation to companies and entrepreneurs. This has an influence on the taxable basis but can also have an indirect effect on the attribution of the right to tax, as an income can only be allocated while the fixed base exists. When a fixed base is closed and income is received late, one can ask oneself how it is to be allocated. Indeed, how can an income arising from an activity which itself would be allocated to a fixed base, be allocated to one which no longer exists?

The second difference relates to establishing the taxable income. I do not know what the case is in other countries, but in France with respect to individuals carrying on professional activities, certain expenses and even sometimes the profits themselves are estimated.

To conclude, I would like to say that Articles 14 and 24 should be modified with respect to the above issues, although this must be done in such a way as to preserve the specificity of professional activities. In particular, the issue as to the application of the arm's length principle to activities carried out in different places by one person in the course of his professional activity must be raised.

The third example – the law firm

David Oliver:
What I propose to do is to take you through examples 3 & 4. I think Mr. Lüthi has some comments to make on example 3 and then we shall be throwing it open to comments and discussions from the floor. Of course the panellists may have something to add in response to the audience's comments or questions. Let us proceed straight away to example three. Let me briefly describe the facts to you. We have a firm of lawyers which practises in Ruritania and all of its partners are resident there. It decides to open a branch office in Utopia and one partner is sent there together with an assistant. The partner who goes to Utopia

remains a partner in the Ruritanian firm and retains his entitlement to a share of the profits in the firm. But of course he is now resident in Utopia. The Utopian office is, for quite a period, in a business development mode. In fact the costs of running the Utopian office are quite high and the fee income which might be said to be attributable to it is quite low. So there is a loss. Of course the partner who is resident in Utopia will be liable in Utopia by reason of his residence to tax in Utopia on his share of the profits. But what about the partners who are in Ruritania? They would say that the income attributable to the fixed base was in fact a loss so they have no liability in Utopia because each of them has a loss. But if you were to import Article 7(2) into Article 14 you might then find an argument being mounted that you should treat the Utopian office as being wholly independent, dealing at arm's length with the Ruritanian head office, and that it might be appropriate to attribute some sort of profit to the Utopian office. So that is the question. It is posed because it will be familiar to a number of people from professional firms who have set up overseas offices.

Daniel Lüthi:
You see the example and you have seen that in Ruritania there is a taxable profit of 100, and you may have figured out, because you have had your coffee now, that formerly the profits must have been 130 and by taking into account the loss then the amount taxable is 100. And so the question in such a situation is whether the principles laid down in Article 7 are applicable in respect of the allocation of the profits or not. So if these principles are applicable, then one can say that there should not be any major problems because you follow a separate entity approach according to Article 7 and the loss in Utopia is then attributed to the partners in Ruritania. Naturally one has to bear in mind that even under Article 7, in 7(2) or 7(3), there may be different views about the amount of dollars in both countries or about expenses to be allocated to Utopia or to Ruritania. But, in general, we assume that these problems can be solved. On the other hand, if you have a situation that lays down that the principles in Article 7 are not applicable, then one comes to the conclusion that in such a situation in Utopia the domestic law will be applied and this might mean that this country has its own attribution rules and that these attribution rules may result in a situation where the loss according to those rules is much lower, with the result again that in Ruritania they might say we do not accept such a lower loss, the loss is still at 30, or in Utopia they might say there is not a loss at all, we think that there is a profit of 10 or 20, so this may then result in double taxation and this is just a problem that may exist in this situation. It is therefore very important that if one comes to the conclusion that Article 14 should be kept, that one

exactly says what rules are applicable with respect to the allocation of profits and the allocation of expenses, and so on.

The fourth example – the law firm assigning a partner to another country

David Oliver:
In example 4 we have again a firm of lawyers practising in Ruritania who decide to assign a partner to Utopia. The Ruritanian partnership has just an association with a firm of lawyers in Utopia and the firm of lawyers in Utopia agree to make office accommodation available to the partner who has been assigned from the Ruritanian partnership. So let us assume that this constitutes a fixed base. In this example the Ruritanian partner who is in Utopia is able to recover costs by charging his time to clients for advice given to them. So we are now into a profit situation in Utopia. How is that profit taxed in Utopia? It is the income attributable to the fixed base – we know that, but is that income taxed by Utopia as income of the partner who is in Utopia, whose activities, you might say, are directly giving rise to the profit, or is it spread among all the partners? Remember we are talking here of a partnership that is totally transparent. This brings up the question as to what is meant by 'his activities' in the context of the 'fixed base regularly available to him ... for the purpose of performing his activities'. The partner based in Utopia might say: 'The activities are not my activities – I am the partner who is here in Utopia.' But on the other hand, in a partnership, does not one partner act on behalf of the other partners as well as for himself? So my view, and I would be interested in comments from the floor, would be that when Article 14 talks about his activities, it does not mean activities simply personal to himself but the activities in which, as a partner of the firm, he is involved – and they are the activities of his fellow partners and the activities of his employees. Supposing also that in the previous example I mentioned that the lawyer who had gone to Utopia had gone there with an assistant. Supposing also now that the partner in Utopia decides to return to Ruritania. He has to go back for sick leave, or for an operation. He goes back to Ruritania for nine months and he is not replaced. He leaves his assistant behind in Utopia. The assistant continues the activities of the fixed base. But do you say that there are no activities attributable to the fixed base because now there is no partner in Ruritania? I do not think so. I think that sort of test is a good one to apply to see just what is meant by 'his activities'. So my conclusion in this case is that it is not only the partner who is in Utopia but also the partners who are in Ruritania who are to be taxed on the income, because it is their activities so to speak

collectively that are giving rise to the income attributable to the fixed base. There are of course, just me let mention, one or two ways which may avoid this. Briefly let us go to example 4(ii) and in this case, we make sure that the partner who is assigned to Utopia ceases to be a partner and what we do is that we put him in the position of being an employee of the Utopian partnership. The Utopian partnership is very cooperative; it grants an employment to this partner who now therefore becomes an employee of the Utopian partnership. The Utopian partnership then just charges a fee to the Ruritanian partnership to cover the cost. Alternatively, the Ruritanian partnership could, for example, have set up a service company in Utopia which could have performed the same function. Another solution might be as shown in example 4(iii) which is based on an IRS letter ruling. Now this is where we had a German partnership, with German partners and a partner in the US. Under the letter ruling the German partnership revised its partnership agreement so as to allocate all of the profits of the US office to the US resident partner – a sort of profit allocation, if you like, in the agreement. And the partner resident in the US filed US returns, reporting his income while the non-resident partners under the agreement were able to say that they were not liable to tax in the US. This is actually going contrary to what I was saying in the previous example because it is not saying that one partner acts on behalf of all. It is actually allowing the profit allocation here to imagine that the US partner is only acting for himself. In a way, I think that the best rationale for this approach is that the US partner actually ceases to be a partner in the partnership, he is like a sole trader, a sole practitioner and the German partnership exists separately. But there is also a more interesting impression which would have already crossed your minds. If the US partner is entitled to the US profits, what happens if there is a good year in the US and what happens if there is a bad year in the US? Somewhere in this there is presumably some equalization method between the US partner and the German partners by way of a cap or a floor or something, because otherwise there are going to be some unhappy partners around according to the fluctuation of the profits.

Rosemarie Portner:
The panellists described the difference between a permanent establishment on the one hand and a fixed base on the other hand and described the various aspects. In my view, an additional aspect could be attributed or added to that. Both provisions, Article 7 on the one hand and Article 14 on the other hand, prescribe that the activity is rendered either through a permanent establishment or carried out through a permanent establishment or rendered as personal services through a fixed place. But a permanent establishment may be maintained even by machines or even pipelines. A permanent establishment does not

require individuals to carry out commercial or industrial activities. On the other hand, in my view, independent personal services require necessarily an individual rendering personal services and there I see another difference between a permanent establishment and a fixed base.

Arvid Skaar:
I fully agree of course that the starting point for the whole discussion is that Article 14 and Article 7 apply to different business activities – so there will always be different business activities and I agree fully that in some cases you will have a permanent establishment even if you do not have any personal services.

David Ward:
I have a question for the panel. Assuming, and perhaps David Oliver's last example is the best one to use, that the partner in the fixed base from time to time may render service to the partnership in Germany and there is an inter-branch charge for that service, or the partnership in Germany might render service to the office in the US with an inter-branch charge. One would assume that the point could be made that a partnership could not deal with itself and the inter-branch charge should be ignored but that would, if Article 7(2) is to be applied, appear to conflict with Article 7(2). The Commentary and the OECD paper on determination of the profits of a permanent establishment seem to concentrate on transfers of goods and not services. In respect of services, it seems to focus on ancillary services to indicate that those should only be charged at cost. These are not ancillary services because these services are by their very nature the essence of the business of the partnership and therefore the question is whether in assessing the income of the partnership in Germany or the income of the partnership in the US, inter-branch billings should be taken into account and deducted in the one case and included in income in the other.

Jacques Sasseville:
I am not sure that I would necessarily agree that the Commentary on Article 7 which incorporates the conclusions of the report on Attribution of Income of Permanent Establishments, generally assumes that services are to be charged at cost. It is really an issue that depends on the answer to the question that you find in paragraph 17.2. It is whether the expense has been incurred for purposes of performing a function, the direct purpose of which relates to the profit generating activity or not or simply to the reduction of the overall costs of the group. Services that would be rendered in relation to a particular file, I would presume would fall within the category where there would be a cost plus mark up. Therefore a profit should be given to the entity that renders the services to the

other one. Those are not management services. I would read the paragraph that generally states that services should be charged strictly on a cost basis as restricted to the circumstances of services relating to internal management or to management of the group as a whole other than income producing services or should I say immediately income producing services as opposed to indirect income producing services. I hope that makes sense.

Michael Waters:
Just to say that if it was a fixed base in the UK, which was providing a service to the rest of the partnership based in Germany, then first of all we would certainly be interested in a recharge with, in appropriate circumstances, a profit element. Of course the fallback position would be that the cost of the activity carried on by the UK partnership for Germany was not an expense incurred wholly and exclusively for the purpose of the UK fixed base and we would strike out as a deduction the cost of providing the service to the rest of the partnership in Germany which would produce the same result as reimbursement of cost where we bring in the receipt. So there is more than one way of approaching the issue.

David Ward:
May I just respond to that and point out that the services are rendered by a partner and a partner is not being paid a salary, so the point about disallowing the expense does not arise in these circumstances, because in the inter-branch charges in the example that David Oliver describes the personnel are partners that are rendering these services and not employees.

David Oliver:
What struck me very much in approaching these examples is that you have to pause and ask yourself whether in discussing the role of Article 14 you should really be looking at the particular sort of activities that are covered by Article 14 and you should therefore not be misled by reason of the fact that Article 14 causes difficulties for particular taxpayers – in other words for partnerships. The same problems could arise under Article 7 and Article 5 for a partnership and those were discussed in Cannes last year. Therefore one needs to keep in mind that, in looking at these problems, one may need to separate the problems that are attributable to the form in which the activity is carried on, through a partnership for example, and the activity itself.

Overall, I am something of a conservative and I would be happy to keep Article 14. It could do with some improvements. I think there were some points that Mr. Thiria made, particularly in relation to Article 24(3) and to the calculation of the income under Article 14, which are very valid.

To What Extent Do Employees Assigned to a Subsidiary Constitute a Permanent Establishment of the Parent Company?

Jacques Sasseville:
The second topic is to what extent employees who are assigned to subsidiaries constitute a permanent establishment for the parent company.[1] The relevance of the topic depends very much on the tax consequences of having a permanent establishment for the parent that would result from sending an employee to a subsidiary. That is something that we will address later so we are not ignoring that issue but you could immediately conclude that the impact might be either on the employee or on the parent company or it might be on both and there are risks that also relate to the fact that even if you have a permanent establishment and think that not much income would be attributed to that permanent establishment, the source country would use the permanent establishment that they would consider to exist to allocate perhaps a little bit more income than they should. So these issues we shall explore later.

The way we are going to proceed is that we are going to focus on one particular example. It is very simply stated that you have a parent company that will send an employee and the employee will work in premises belonging to a subsidiary.[2] The example that we will be using is on the overhead No. 4.[3] This example raises most of the issues that are addressed in a paper I think was distributed to you.[4] So I shall simply state the facts. You have a senior accountant who is employed by a parent company who is sent to review the accounting practices of a newly acquired subsidiary. He realizes that there is a lot of work to do. So he will spend quite a lot of time, but he will be moving from office to office in the subsidiary's headquarters. After an initial review, he decides to implement changes in the accounting practices of the subsidiary. He has a very broad mandate to do that and in that process he arranges for the subsidiary to acquire various products and services from the parent company, for example

1. *See* background note in Appendix 2.
2. *See* Appendix 2, Overhead Nos. 1–3.
3. *See* Appendix 2, Overhead No. 4.
4. Reproduced in Appendix 2.

the accounting software that is used throughout the multinational. A management fee equal to 115% of his salary will be charged by the parent to the subsidiary.

So the issue is whether there will be a permanent establishment of the parent company. There are two aspects that we will consider. First, whether the general rules of permanent establishment, what I call the fixed place of business concept of permanent establishment, apply.[5] The second aspect is whether the dependent agent rules that deem a permanent establishment to exist in certain circumstances could apply. That is overhead No. 6.[6] Let us focus on the various questions you would have to address in trying to determine whether or not the employee will constitute a fixed place of business, a permanent establishment. The first question is what is the business of the parent company that is carried on in the offices of the headquarters of the subsidiary.

Arvid Skaar:
I have some sympathy for this person and I would very much like to get him out of trouble. So the first question would be whether the activity he is performing is a business activity under the treaty, because if it is not, we do not have any problems and we can all go home. The second question is, if we have a business activity, whose business activity is it? Is it the parent company's business activity or is the subsidiary's activity? For the first question, I would say that if this person was merely engaged in record keeping etc., it is clear that he would not be performing a business activity. That would be an ancillary activity that would be accepted under the treaties. But it seems from the description here that this person is engaged in some sort of managerial accounting and that would be a part of a business activity and so there is no way out of it in that respect. The question whether or not this is the activity of the parent company is more difficult. I would say that his problems could easily be avoided simply by concluding an employment contract between the subsidiary and the senior accountant so that he was an employee of the subsidiary. This may not always be the case if there is a serious case of mismanagement and the parent company has to try and get everything on wheels again. That might be different. But in general, I would think that multinational companies would avoid problems in this field by making this person an employee of the subsidiary. We could also ask, what if this was not a person from the parent company? It could have been a senior accountant from Price Waterhouse. Would he then be performing the

5. *See* Appendix 2, Overhead No. 5.
6. *See* Appendix 2, Overhead No. 6.

business activity of the parent company or not? I would say that he would not be performing the activity of the parent company.

David Oliver:
I would just like to make one or two further comments because the point that arises here is that the employment is not transferred from the parent company to the subsidiary. The example assumes that the employment remains with the parent company. Now there are a large number of reasons why somebody being assigned for a short period to another company in a group to perform a task does not have his employment transferred and most of those reasons have nothing to do with taxation whatsoever. They will relate to the pension entitlement or any other benefit entitlements of the employee. They will relate maybe to the terms for the termination of his employment contract, the period of notice he can expect to receive, the compensation he could expect to receive if his employment contract was terminated, the simple hassle, as we would say in English, of actually moving an employment from one company to another. And, of course, for that reason, some companies have a single company within the group which employs all the employees and simply charges out to subsidiaries for their services. So those are considerations which have to be taken into account here in looking to see whether it is in fact the business of the parent company that is wholly or partly carried on through this fixed place of business, if indeed there is a fixed place of business, because the normal thing that might happen in such circumstances is simply that the costs of employment would be recharged.

I also think that it is important to bear in mind here what, if I may say so, is a classic OECD Model aspect of the example, in that it refers to a parent company and a subsidiary. You might want to contemplate what the position would be if it was not a parent company and subsidiary but a parent company and a sub-subsidiary or a subsidiary and a sister subsidiary, because I think as the discussion develops we will see that some of the issues in this particular example turn on the management role of the parent company.

Jacques Sasseville:
The only point I would add to that is the issue of the employment contract. Given that there will be a management fee, I think you should not pay too much attention to the employment contract. If it is shifted to the subsidiary, the employee becomes formally an employee of the subsidiary. How do you justify the payment of the management fee for the services? You might have to go beyond the legal arrangement and look at the functions that are performed to see whether there is a business of the parent being carried out. But assuming that we agree that in that scenario there is a business of the parent that is carried on by

the employee, then we look at whether we can say that those activities are performed through a fixed place of business. And here the question that we would have to look at is whether the number of different offices that will be used by the employee in the same building constitute one place of business. In other words, for there to be a sufficient geographical link, do we need to identify a few square metres and can there not be more than one office?

The *Alphawell* case – the right to use facilities

Arvid Skaar:
Perhaps this issue could be illustrated by a recent Supreme Court case from Norway. The case was about a UK resident taxpayer, Mr. Pegrum. He was based in Wales. He worked for a Norwegian oil company, Statoil, and he had a rather long history with them. He had been employed there prior to working as a consultant in his own company and he had then chosen to be an employee of his own company, namely Alphawell. The contract between the oil company and Alphawell said that he should be available for the oil company nine months every year. He could work either in Norway or in Wales. For some reason, he seemed to work a little bit less than 183 days in Norway every year except for one year when he counted wrongly I think. And what happened is that the Norwegian tax authorities wanted to tax the company, Alphawell, for a permanent establishment in Norway.

In the beginning, the company was taxed for the whole of its income including the income related to work performed in Wales. The taxpayer had to go all the way to the appeal court in Norway (not the Supreme Court) to convince the tax authorities that this was wrong. So before the Supreme Court there was only the issue of whether or not there was a permanent establishment for the activity performed in Norway. There were of course a number of contentions but the thing that made the deepest impression on the Court was the fact that he stayed for a little bit more than 600 days in Norway in the course of 4 years and split across 50 visits. In addition to that he worked at different locations. For one project he would be in this building, the next project in another building and this would go on like that. He also went to another city twice. And the taxpayer's attorney said in the Supreme Court that his client even had to sit behind the coffee machine for a period of time, as if it is impossible to get a permanent establishment behind a coffee machine. Anyway, the Court did not buy that argument but they bought his case so they found that this was not a permanent establishment. The reason seemed to be that there were so many interruptions in his stays in Norway and there were so many different locations – he was sitting here and there in a huge office complex and this was not consistent with the word 'fixed' because he was moved around so much. My personal feeling is that this may result in a strange sort of tax advice in Norway from now on because you have to advise people not to use the same desk for a long period of time. Actually the best advice is not to sit down at all. But anyway we have that case and it has something to do with the senior accountant although we do not know exactly where the limit lies. The accountant will probably stay in the same building – perhaps that would be OK for the Supreme Court in Norway too.

Philippe Thiria:
I would like to add only one brief comment. I am always nervous of fixing borders in relation to an economic agent's behaviour. We will come back to this in the fourth point relating to the duration of stay.

As for measuring above which frequency changes of offices begin to have effect, I think that it is best to take a pragmatic approach. The following questions should be asked: Why does he move? Why does he have several offices? Would other people in the same situation, but who do not come across territoriality problems, do the same? I think that this approach is to be preferred, as it should be as regards permanent establishments. Fixing borders actually may do more to encourage fraud than to help taxpayers solve their specific problems.

Jacques Sasseville:
That shows that the problems we are looking at here are broader than problems simply related to subsidiary and parent though they could arise more frequently in the case of a parent-subsidiary relationship. On that particular issue of the permanent establishment, whether you could have a choice between a fixed square metre approach or a broader concept, the one example we have discussed in one of our working groups was that of a professional drug dealer who would be in a park and would be forced by police activities to move from tree to tree. And the issue was whether that would be a permanent establishment, even though he is never using the same part of the park and someone pointed out that he would certainly consider that as his place of business if someone tried to do the same thing in his park. The next question we have to look at is an interesting one because I would not have thought that it would arise, but the question is, should the parent company have a legally forceable right to use the offices or rather should the simple fact that the office is used be enough?

Arvid Skaar:
This may not be a particularly practical issue for this senior accountant as there is a parent-subsidiary issue. But it seems in practice that there are some differ-

ences between countries in the world on what kind of right of use the taxpayer should have in the fixed place of business. Is it enough that he just uses it factually or does he have to have some sort of right to use it? And there is a case in Germany, and I think Germany here is quite an exception, although they have invented and developed the notion of permanent establishment. There is a case from 1990 where a Swiss consultancy firm was held not to have a permanent establishment in Germany because they only used the client's facilities and they did not have a right to use it. If you say that it is sufficient if you factually use the fixed place of business, then you could be out there on the streets doing whatever, and you would still have a permanent establishment. I think that the Supreme Court in Germany has somehow modified this decision in later decisions but it is still an issue. I do not think it is a particularly important issue in respect of the parent/subsidiary case because it is so easy to circumvent any conclusions here.

The length or frequency of use

Jacques Sasseville:
The next question is really the crucial one, I think. How long should the employee use the offices or how frequently should these offices be used for them to constitute a permanent establishment?

Michael Waters:
This a bit like the point which I mentioned in connection with Article 14 concerning the writer with a research project which of its nature could be over and done with inside a month. The question was about whether one should conclude merely from the fact that the duration was short that it could not have been a fixed base; or whether one should have regard to the fact that one month was totally sufficient to complete the entire project because it was of its nature only of short duration. And this illustrates the sort of difficulties that tax authorities have in deciding how long a fixed place of business should exist before in practice it is regarded as a permanent establishment. Article 5 has no firm indicator on this, nor has the Commentary. One might conclude that a very short period should not be counted, purely as a practical administrative measure. It is not likely that very much money will be attributable to a permanent establishment which only lasts for a short period of time and that might be a working hypothesis. Some people speak in terms of 6 months as a rough and ready arbitrary dividing line. But I was reminded then of when I was in the Slovak Republic a year or two ago, on an OECD training course, taking Slovak tax officials through the OECD model. It turned out that they had great problems in

working out the taxation consequences when a UK company sent staff to work in a particular business in Bratislava. This happened to be a growth industry in Bratislava and some fortunate UK company had the contract for providing staff and the UK company made sure that they each spent less than six months in Bratislava. One reason for that was to help the employees escape Slovak tax under Article 15(2). The Slovaks were very interested in considering whether they could regard the employees as constituting a permanent establishment of the UK company which had the contract to provide the staff. That illustrates three things. First of all, the issues we are considering need not be between related companies. Second, we are dealing with practical issues which are causing enormous interest particularly in the countries of the former Soviet Union. Third, if you have a fixed rule of saying that there is no permanent establishment if employees are in a country for less than six months, that may not deal with the facts and circumstances of a particular case like the one the Slovak authorities were considering. One also has to consider, I think, paragraph 3 of Article 5 in the OECD model. This says that a building site constitutes a PE only if it lasts more than 12 months. There may be a clear implication there that without that paragraph a building site that lasted for, say, 11 months might well be a PE. So one might conclude that there is a time limit less than 12 months which gives you a permanent establishment. But many treaties that the UK has entered into have, at the request of the treaty partner, a much lower threshold. We have a number of treaties where we have agreed that a building site can be a PE if it lasts for more than six months. Now that might carry the implication that, without that six month time limit for building sites, a building site could be a PE if it lasted for less than six months. That seems to be the unspoken acknowledgement of having only a six month time limit in paragraph 3 of Article 5. So for all these reasons I do not think it is very easy to say for certain that there is a minimum period before one has a permanent establishment. I think that one can say broadly that the chances are that most countries would say anything longer than six months is a permanent establishment. On the other hand something less than six months may be a permanent establishment depending on the facts and circumstances, which is probably about as unhelpful as you would expect a tax authority to be.

Agency permanent establishment

Jacques Sasseville:
Just before we deal with this second aspect, there was one issue we did not discuss. It is whether paragraph 2 of Article 5 could be relevant. You will

remember that paragraph 2 of Article 5 lists certain things that are considered to be permanent establishments. It reads as follows: 'the term permanent establishment includes especially (a) a place of management, (b) a branch, (c) an office...' and the issue there is whether the parent company is carrying on business through its employee in an office, even though the office belongs to the subsidiary. Is that not automatically a permanent establishment regardless of the interesting discussion on the time period? One answer to that is that you have to read paragraph 2 in the light of paragraph 1 and that is purely indicated in paragraph 12 of the Commentary on Article 5. So the issue of the time still arises even if you look at 'office' and you conclude that because the accountant is using an office, that is the end of the questions. The other point is the reference to 'place of management.' A place of management is automatically a permanent establishment if it meets also the conditions of paragraph 1. Well, the accountant is working in the headquarters of the subsidiary. That is a place of management – certainly a place of management for the subsidiary. And the question here is when we refer to place of management in Article 5, is that a place of management of the enterprise to which we want to attribute the PE or a place of management of any enterprise? For example, if you are a big hotel chain, you have hotels in different countries and you send some employees to act as managers of other hotels which belong to subsidiaries. They do not constitute themselves permanent establishments for you. The fact that your managers will be doing management – would that automatically constitute a place of management? One of the OECD working groups that has looked at that, has concluded that you can only use this reference to place of management in relation to management of the enterprise to which you want to attribute a PE – not any kind of management of anyone. Having said that, let us now focus on the agency permanent establishment again based on those facts that we have described at the beginning of this topic. In order to conclude that there would be an agency permanent establishment as commented in paragraph 5 of Article 5 of the OECD Model Tax Convention, there are various questions that you would have to address. The first one would be, is the accountant acting in the name of the parent company?

Arvid Skaar:
Again this is a question of the business activity performed by the agent. And since the agency rule of Article 5(5) does not have any specific business activity test, the same rules would apply to the agency as we have already discussed. So the senior accountant will be faced with the same issue – is he performing the business of the parent company or is he performing the business of the subsidiary? This may well depend on the circumstances.

Jacques Sasseville:
In that particular set of circumstances, I personally would be inclined to see a business of the parent company which is the business of managing its subsidiaries. The next question would be – does the accountant have an authority to conclude contracts on the basis of those facts?

Philippe Thiria:
Indeed, the following question should be raised: does the accountant acting as dependent agent have the power to conclude contracts?

Let us attempt to examine different hypotheses.

If the accountant's mission is purely technical, it is unlikely that it will lead to a second contract granting the accountant authority or power in the subsidiary.

However, if the mission relates to the management of the company, in particular with the subsidiary's directors, then the task carried out by the accountant would have required a written contract had the parent and subsidiary companies been independent legal persons.

For example: an accountant examines the subsidiary's situation, reaches a diagnosis and concludes that the subsidiary has needs. Going further, he suggests measures to meet those needs. He can then decide to prolong his stay in the subsidiary in order to take the necessary measures and, in this case, this is a second mission which he gives himself. He can also decide that the subsidiary is to purchase either the goods or services from the parent company which might meet the needs thus determined. In both cases, if the financial conditions of the purchases were also set between the accountant and the subsidiary, there is an implicit contract between the parent and the subsidiary under which the parent supplies the goods or necessary services or prolongs the accountant's stay. It is important to note that this implicit contract is not always written and that, quite often, its existence is not even noticed by the parties in question.

In this case, therefore, there are two superimposed contracts. The first, for the first period of examination of the situation – this is an 'assignment' ('*détachement*' in French) contract between the parent and the subsidiary. The second, which is concluded in so far as the accountant has the authority required in order to do so, and which follows the first contract.

An issue therefore arises as regards documents: have the real contracts been identified as such, and, if so, were they drawn up in writing?

Three aspects of this issue must be examined. Firstly, the legal aspect, as contracts signed between the parent and the subsidiary often must be authorized by certain public authorities. Next, the tax audit: one must be able to describe what the service consists of and what its price is. Lastly, this is of course a transfer pricing issue, as throughout this whole examination we have been constantly coming across the issue of transfer pricing.

It is therefore after having analysed the real nature of explicit and implicit contracts that one can address the issue of knowing whether it is the accountant who concluded them himself and whether he had the requisite power to do so, as in this case it would therefore be legal power.

Jacques Sasseville:
On the principles I think I would agree with Mr. Thiria. I have a question, however, and that would be if that is exactly what happens, there are various services and products which are sent from the parent to the subsidiary. For example, the accountant has been told that he has the power to do that and he gets someone to bring a copy of the software used by the group to the subsidiary. He installs that and he gets a number of colleagues to come and give some training as to how the software works. And he gets a number of colleagues to come and make sure that there are no bugs, etc. That service is provided but there is no charge for that. All you get at the end is a management fee of 115% of the salary of the accountant. Then a few years later, there is a tax auditor who comes, he looks at that, he has just read the transfer pricing guidelines and he makes an adjustment for the services and the software. Would you then be able to conclude that there were contracts concluded even if there has not been any payment, that it was following a transfer pricing adjustment that a charge for tax purposes was made? So you would then say that there were no contracts concluded? The fact is that you still have the services and the software but there has been no consideration – do you not require a transfer followed by a consideration? But then that raises problems of how tax is then compatible with other branches of law. So that is a question I would raise and I would not expect anyone to provide any answer.

The next question concerns whether he has the authority to conclude contracts – are these contracts related to a business of the parent company?

Daniel Lüthi:
There are in fact I think two arguments that could be developed to show that there is no agency establishment. The first argument would be based on paragraph 40 of the Commentary on Article 5 paragraph 7. There it is said that managerial and supervisory functions performed by the parent company for its subsidiary do not constitute a permanent establishment for the parent. One could argue that the review of accounting practices and the measures you take as in the example constitute such functions. Then naturally one would also have to draw the conclusion that there is no permanent establishment. Another argument could be developed based on paragraph 33 of the Commentary where it is said

that the authority to conclude contracts must cover contracts which constitute the business proper of the parent and the Commentary afterwards distinguishes between so-called business contracts and internal contracts. There the question arises whether it is the business of the parent company to sell services in the accounting area also to other companies, or whether it is just part of the functions of the parent or of the shareholders, so to say, to perform such services. So if one would conclude that such an activity is an internal one and has nothing to do with the main business activity of the parent towards third parties, then one would again conclude that there is no permanent establishment.

Jacques Sasseville:
The last question is, and it is the crucial one here – is the authority to conclude contracts habitually exercised?

Arvid Skaar:
This is a question that could also be illustrated by the *Alphawell* case. Because in that case, after having lost on the fixed place of business issue, the tax authorities argued that as Mr. Pegrum was the only employee of the company, he had to conclude all the contracts of the company. So he concluded the first one, the original contract, and then he renewed this contract three times. So altogether he signed four times in the period of four years. The question was whether this was enough for an habitual exercise of the authority. The Supreme Court said that in a case where this is merely renewal, merely repeating the original contracts, this would not be sufficient and I think that is also consistent with the doctrine elsewhere. It is a required regularity but in *Alphawell* there was no question of new contracts. In our case, with the senior accountant, we would have to look at how many times he has done this and for how long, and I am not sure that we really know that for certain but it seems to me that he is within range of a permanent establishment as far as this condition is concerned. But then again I think multinational companies would easily avoid the problem simply by telling him that it is in order to persuade them to buy these things but do not conclude any contracts. You just ask him to call George in the home office and he will do the rest. So I think that it is an easy way out for those who think that this may cause problems.

Jacques Sasseville:
The last two issues are really addressing the consequences of the finding of a permanent establishment. What income would be taxable in the home State in relation to the parent company, and of course, what are the tax consequences for the employee?

Philippe Thiria:
This is a very complex and broad subject and this is no doubt not the place to fully discuss it. The main consequences can simply be outlined. In your questions, you could possibly direct us towards other issues.

Let us first examine the point of view of the company itself and in particular the taxable result of the permanent establishment.

Where there are transactions with third parties, i.e. where the dependent agent intervened in order to represent the parent company in transactions with third parties, we are faced with the typical issue of attributing to the permanent establishment the profits which accrue to it.

However, we are examining a different issue: that in which services are performed by the parent to the subsidiary. We shall distinguish between profits and expenses: the profits will be the arm's length prices of services performed in favour of the subsidiary; the expenses will be comprised of the cost of the employee and other expenses related to his activity as well as the expenditure incurred by the parent company in relation to this performance of services. This case does not give rise to any problems in establishing the taxable income. However, this situation entails cumbersome administrative obligations attached to the existence of the permanent establishment: distinct accounts must be kept, tax returns must be completed without forgetting the possible risks attached to the force of attraction of the permanent establishment over a certain amount of other income which the parent company might receive from the State of the subsidiary.

Let us now examine the tax consequences for the employee. Either his employment conditions make him a resident of the State of the subsidiary, on the basis of Article 15, and in this case there is no problem: he will be taxed normally in accordance with the rules in force in this State. Alternatively he is not considered to be a resident of the State of the subsidiary but, for example, a resident of the State of the parent company. In this case, one must refer to the three conditions set out in Article 15(2) of the Model Treaty. As you know, these are:

1) duration of 183 days;
2) obligation for the remuneration to be paid by a non-resident, and
3) this remuneration must not be borne by a permanent establishment of the parent in the State of the subsidiary.

It is obvious that in all our hypotheses, we have a permanent establishment. Consequently, the third condition will not be fulfilled and, in this case also, the employee assigned abroad will be taxed in the State of the subsidiary.

One consequence which has already been raised by Mr. Oliver is that the employee is a tax subject of the State of the subsidiary, although in all of his relations concerning social protection and labour law, he views himself as the employee of the parent company. It is clear that it is by means of salary negotiations that all of the difficulties arising from this situation might be solved.

To conclude, there are no detrimental consequences.

Chairman:
Am I right to conclude that only under very exceptional circumstances an employee sent to a subsidiary will constitute a permanent establishment of the parent company, but it may happen and one should be aware of this possibility?

Jacques Sasseville:
Only in very exceptional circumstances would he constitute an agency permanent establishment. I would probably not agree with the 'very exceptional circumstances' in the case of the fixed place of business permanent establishment. Depending on what other observations there are, that would be my final observation.

Comments from the audience

Peter Sundgren (Sweden):
The book written by Professor Skaar – a 500 page dissertation – has a very simple title: 'Permanent Establishment'. But it also has a very intriguing subtitle. It says 'The Erosion of a Tax Treaty Principle'. Having listened to the discussions today, I think you have a point there. If the Supreme Court of Norway is called upon to consider the consequences on the permanent establishment question of someone standing behind a coffee machine, I do think you have a point. I should just like to repeat also to the members of the OECD that the business and industry advisory committee (BIAC) to the OECD has made a suggestion which I think is very helpful in trying to reduce the number of cases where the question of permanent establishment can arise at all, in suggesting that small permanent establishments should be taxed only in the country of residence. It is also a suggestion made, I think, in the European Community. The treaty negotiators in Denmark and Sweden have also foreseen the difficulties that might arise with a permanent establishment with regard to the Ureson Bridge and declaring in the treaty that all activities concerned with that bridge should also only be taxed in the country of residence. I shall come back to you on that in BIAC and the OECD so we can carry on these discussions.

Michael Waters (United Kingdom):
I would be interested to know if your article covers a couple of points on this subject which intrigue me and to which I do not know the answers. One concerns issues of fragmentation. If the permanent establishment approaches this threshold of 3.5m ECU, whether profits or turnover, can it then split into two or three separate permanent establishments to keep below the threshold? Second, is this a good approach if the enterprise is a resident of a State which operates the exemption method of eliminating double taxation since it, under domestic law perhaps and certainly under a treaty, might not tax the permanent establishment either, so it is not taxed anywhere? And what happens if the permanent establishment grows in size after a few years? If your threshold is based on turnover and in the early years the permanent establishment by normal arm's length measure has incurred a loss, will the State where the permanent establishment is situated still be obliged to give relief for that loss in a later year even though it would not, under your suggestion if it is based on turnover, have been able to tax a profit?

Kees van Raad (Netherlands):
I readily agree with those members of the panel who believe that, in reality, the requirements for assuming an agency permanent establishment will rarely arise in the meaning that truly contracts are concluded in the name of the enterprise. I would like to ask a question to those members of the panel who do believe that this case may arise because there is a paragraph in the Commentary on Article 5, paragraph 34 which reads as follows (it is sort of a 'force of attraction' where agency permanent establishment is concerned): 'Where the requirements set out in paragraph 5 are met, a permanent establishment of the enterprise exists to the extent that the person acts for the latter, i.e. not only to the extent that such a person exercises the authority to conclude contracts in the name of the enterprise.' The question concerns the activity of the employee when he is working back in the home office in respect of the job he was going to do abroad. Should the profit attributed to that activity equally be considered a permanent establishment profit in respect of which the employer, the company, is subject to tax in the source country?

Jacques Sasseville:
It would be possible, for example if in carrying out his updating of the software of the subsidiary the accountant has quickly to go back to his own country to get a few instructions or to provide a quick fix to a bug, that this could be related to the activities of the PE because it will relate to the function that is performed. But I think that generally that would not be the case. So we are now talking about very exceptional circumstances in very exceptional cases.

Concluding remarks

Jacques Sasseville:
I just wanted to thank the other panellists who have contributed to the note that has been distributed to you and which explores these issues. I thought that the discussion was very interesting and I certainly appreciated the comments from both the panellists and the audience.

Chairman:
Once again thank you to all of the panellists and in particular to the panellists from the OECD who have come to this congress and who, I hope, will continue to contribute to this type of seminar in future congresses. Further, thanks to all of you as well for attending this discussion and for contributing to it. Having said this, I close the meeting.

Appendix 1: Outline on Article 14*

Allocation of profits under Article 14 of the OECD Model – Should it follow Article 7 or should it be subject to different rules?

Three aspects of Article 14:

1) the persons covered;
2) the fixed base;
3) the attribution of income to the fixed base.

The persons covered

Does Article 14 apply to both individuals (including partnerships) and companies? Compare the US Model which only applies to individuals, the Commentary on the United Nations Model, Mexico's observation in the OECD Commentary (1995 Update para. 4.1) and the deletion in the 1992 Model of the United States reservation in para. 7 of the 1977 Model.

What is the position of hybrids (treated as a company by one State and as a transparent partnership by the other State)?

In principle is there any reason to distinguish between companies and individuals if the services performed are similar?

The fixed base

Per Commentary (para. 4): Not appropriate to try to define 'fixed base' but thought permanent establishment should be reserved for commercial and industrial activities. Compare Article 5(1) which initially defines permanent establishment as 'a fixed place of business' through which the business of the enterprise is wholly or partly carried on.

This definition ('a fixed place of business') (says the Commentary to Article 5 para. 2) contains the following conditions:

* Prepared by David Oliver.

'– the existence of a "place of business", i.e. a facility such as premises or, in certain instances, machinery or equipment;
– this place of business must be "fixed", i.e., it must be established at a distinct place with a certain degree of permanence;
– the carrying on of the business enterprise through this fixed place of business. This means usually that persons who, in one way or another, are dependent on the enterprise (personnel) conduct the business of the enterprise in the State in which the fixed place is situated.'

Fixed base implies:

i) A given location.
ii) Fixed – a *degree* of continuity or permanence: paragraph 4 of the Commentary refers to a 'centre of activity of a fixed or permanent character'.
iii) There must be a connection between the base and the activities – 'for the purpose of performing his activities'.

Possible differences between permanent establishment and fixed base:

1. The fixed base need only be 'regularly available'. The Commentary, as quoted above, refers to a *centre of activity* of a fixed or a permanent character. (Emphasis supplied. Compare the French text which refers to certain traits of fixity or permanence.) This emphasizes that continuity is not required – compare paragraph 7 of the Commentary on Article 5 that permanent establishment activities 'need not be permanent in the sense that there is no interruption of operation, but operations must be carried out on a regular basis'. Does this distinguish the flexible characterization of a professional activity from the much lower level of mobility in a business operation? It is well characterized by the example in the Commentary in Article 14 of a physician's consulting room as constituting a fixed base. The consulting room will be at a given location, it will be used for the purpose of performing the activities, and it will be used with some degree of continuity. However, when the consulting room is not in use by the particular physician it may be hired out to other physicians for their use.

   Compare the position of a consultant travelling frequently to another country to meet local clients there: does he need to have a furnished office at his disposal in order to have a fixed base? Or is any fixed place through which his personal activity may be exercised to be treated as a fixed base (e.g. a hotel room, a client's office, etc.)?
2. A place of business may require to be equipped for the business activity.

There is much greater flexibility in the provision of a base for professional services.

3. Note an interesting decision of the German *Bundesfinanzhof* (14 January 1982) which illustrates circumstances in which permanent establishment and fixed base do not have the same meaning.[1] Paragraph 7 of Article 7 of the German-Swiss treaty provides that a participation in a business association of persons such as a partnership amounts to a permanent establishment. The *Bundesfinanzhof* held that the mere creation, by a German resident and a Swiss resident, of a *professional* partnership which was to operate in Switzerland did not by itself constitute for the German resident a fixed base in Switzerland. The Court based its decision on the ground the Article 14 of the treaty did not contain any provisions similar to Article 7(7). The conclusion was that the terms 'permanent establishment' and 'fixed base' are not identical.
4. The provisions of paras. 3–7 of Article 5 are not mentioned in Article 14: but note US Revenue Ruling 75–131 (French concert performer represented in US by independent agent for purposes of US tour: no fixed base).

Attribution of income

The Commentary to Article 14 (para. 3) states that:

> 'The provisions of the Article are similar to those for business profits and rest in fact on the same principles as those of Article 7. The provisions of Article 7 and the Commentary thereon could therefore be used as guidance for interpreting and applying Article 14.'

Article 14 however only effectively incorporates the provisions of Article 7(1). It can be argued that there is nothing in Article 14 to indicate that the provisions of Article 7(2), (3) and (4) are incorporated into Article 14. There could be good reason for not incorporating them, so as to give greater flexibility for the reasons discussed below. The Commentary itself seems to recognize that paragraph 3 might be an overstatement because it opens paragraph 4 stating 'Even if Articles 7 and 14 are based on the same principles...'. However, there are different views on this point.

Note that Article 14 refers to income while Article 7 refers to profits. Is any difference intended by these different terms? Would income be understood in the

1. *European Taxation* 1982 at 364.

context to refer to net income? Note that Article 24(3) makes no reference to a fixed base.

A fruitful way in which to approach the discussion of issues arising in the allocation of profits under Article 14 is to take a series of examples. We will assume that in each case the States involved have an OECD Model Treaty between them.

Example 1

A writer is resident in Ruritania. She enters into a contract with a publisher in Utopia to write a novel and receives an advance payment. She begins work in Ruritania on the manuscript; the following summer she spends three months in Arcadia, in rented accommodation, continuing her writing and then returns to Ruritania. Finding that she needs to carry out further research in Illyria, for the purpose of the plot, she travels to that country for two months, moving around and staying in various small hotels or private houses. She returns to Ruritania and completes the manuscript.

Example 1

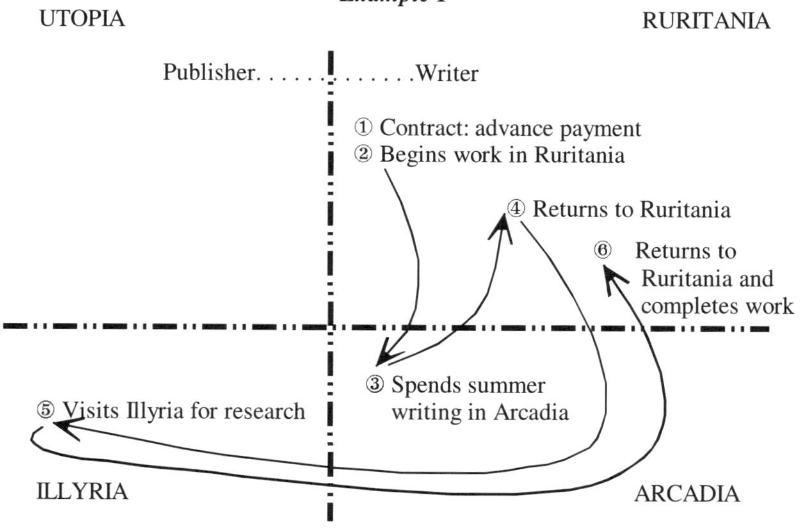

Example 2

An architect practises in Ruritania, where he is a resident. He has two clients in Utopia. The projects in which he is involved for those clients extend over, say, a 3-year period. The two projects are located quite close to one another and he therefore rents an office at a particular location for use as a drawing office etc. and as a base during his visits there which may take place, say, every three or four weeks and last for three or four days at a time.

While the whole of the fee income on the Utopian projects is derived from the Utopian clients, some of the work will have been performed in Ruritania and some part of it is performed during his visits to Utopia. Occasionally, during a visit to Utopia, he has to make a return trip to Ruritania to collect additional information, drawings, etc.

Would the position be different if the architect were employed by his own company and it was that company which was engaged in the activities in Ruritania and Utopia?

Example 2

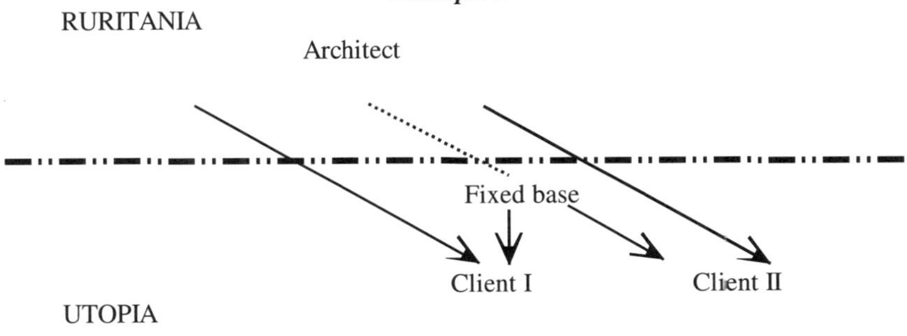

Example 3

A firm of lawyers practises in Ruritania. All its partners are resident in Ruritania. It decides to open a branch office in Utopia. (This activity is permitted, subject to certain restrictions, by the appropriate regulatory authorities.) A partner in the Ruritanian firm is sent to Utopia to partner the new office, together with an assistant solicitor. He remains a partner in the Ruritanian firm and retains his entitlement to a share of the profits in that firm. However, he is now resident in Utopia.

The Utopian office is, for the first few years, in a 'business development' mode. There are substantial costs in running the office and the partner and his assistant have to be compensated for the much higher living costs in Utopia as well as the travel costs of returning to Ruritania, either on business or for holidays. In accounting terms the Utopian office is operating at a loss.

The Utopian resident partner will be liable to tax in Utopia on his share of profits by reason of his resident there. (Let us assume for the moment that Utopia has a credit rather than an exemption system.) Can it be said however that there is, so far as the partnership is concerned, no income (but a loss) attributable to the fixed base?

If Article 7(2) was applied then it might be argued that a distinct and separate enterprise would not incur a loss but, having regard to its activities, would make a small profit.

Example 3

RURITANIA	Partners	Overall partnership profits 100 (including Utopian office)
UTOPIA	Partner	Loss of Utopian office (30)

Example 4

Two firms of lawyers carry on business in partnership in Ruritania and Utopia respectively. They are part of a worldwide 'association' of firms of lawyers but no partner is a partner in the partnership of any other firm. The Ruritanian partnership decides to assign a partner to Utopia. Office accommodation is made available to him by the Utopian partnership. The Ruritanian partner is able to recover costs by charging his time to clients for advice given to them.

As in the previous example, the Ruritanian partner continues to draw his profit share from the Ruritanian firm and again as previously Utopia will tax him in full on his profit share, by reason of residence. However, there is now a profit rather than a loss attributable to the fixed base.

Example 4(i)

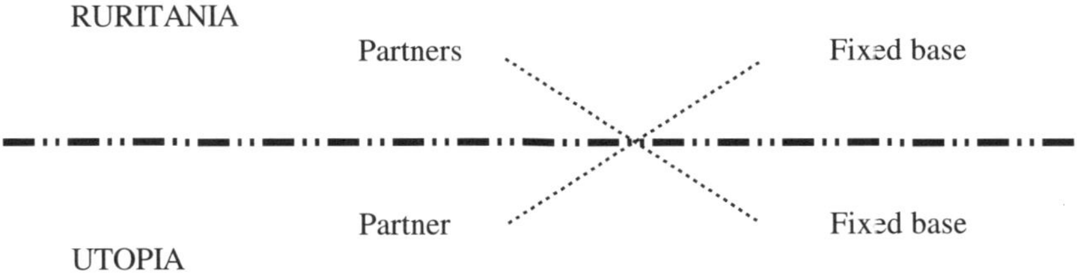

One view of partnership is that it is a business carried on in common by the partners. Each partner binds his fellow partners in the activities in which he engages. The question in this example is this: 'Is the Ruritanian partnership (and thus all the Ruritanian partners) performing duties in Utopia by reason of the activity of the partner in Utopia, or is he the only one who is performing the duties, for the purposes of Article 14?'

If a partnership is within the treaty definition of resident of a contracting State, then it would seem clear that the partnership ('he') is performing its ('his') duties from the fixed base. In such a case (and assuming Utopian domestic law so provides) Utopia may tax the profit of the Utopian office in the hands of the partnership. To the extent that part of this profit forms part of the partnership profit share of the Ruritanian partner, it will not tax that part again since it is already taxing it in the hands of the Ruritanian resident partner by reason of residence.

Is a practical solution to such a problem for the Ruritanian partner to cease to draw any profit share from the Ruritanian partnership and to become an employee of the Utopian partnership which charges back his salary to the Ruritanian partnership? There is then no fixed base in Utopia available to the Ruritanian partnership.

Example 4(ii)

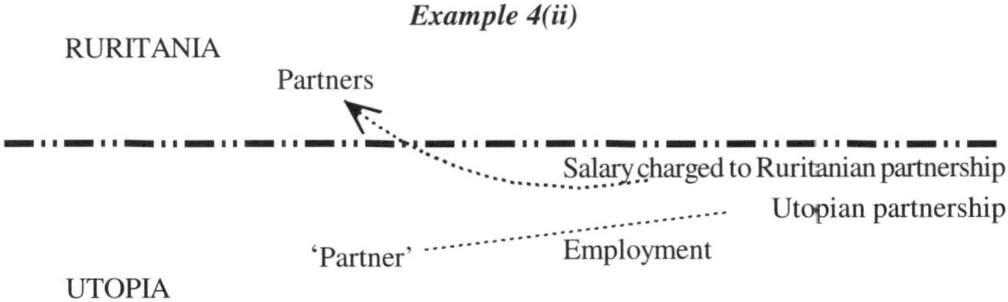

Another solution is suggested by an IRS private letter ruling issued to a German law firm.[2] The German partnership revised its partnership agreement so as to allocate all of the profits of its US office to the US resident partner there. Previously the US partnership had filed US partnership returns reporting the operating results of the activities conducted through the US office. The partner resident in the US filed US returns reporting all of his income while the non-resident partners each filed non-resident tax returns reporting their share of the income from US sources. As a result of the change in the partnership agreement, the IRS ruled that:

1) The German non-US resident partners are not taxable in the United States on their distributive shares, if any, of the partnership's income that is attributable to the partnership's New York branch office and services performed by the resident partner under Article 14 of the US/German income tax treaty.
2) The resident partner is only taxable in the United States on his distributive share of partnership income because he alone performed independent personal services for the partnership in the United States (Article 14).
3) The reporting requirement imposed on each German non-US resident partner of the partnership was waived provided the partnership disclosed the position taken on the US/German treaty for the particular taxable year.

The rationale for the ruling was that because the resident partner only performs services for the partnership in the United States, where he was residing, the partner was only taxable in the United States on his distributive share of partnership income in accordance with Article 14 of the US/German treaty. Furthermore, pursuant to Article 14(1) the income derived by the non-US resident partners in Germany was only taxable in Germany because they did not perform any services in the United States.

Example 4(iii)

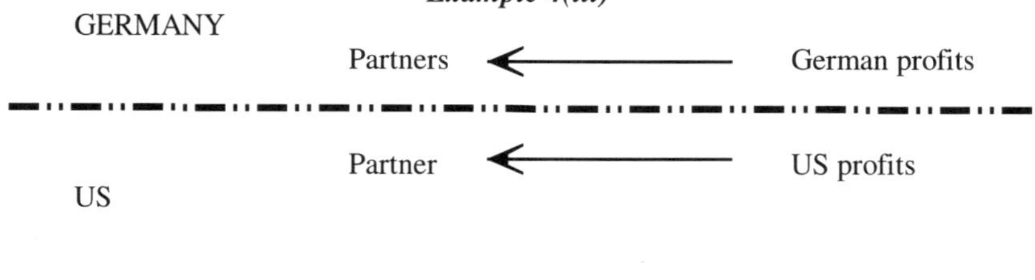

2. IRS Ltr. rl. 9331012, 5 May 1993; discussed in 'Taxation of Professionals' by Sanford H. Goldberg (1994) *Canadian Tax Journal* Vol. 42 No. 2 p. 559.

Conclusions

1) The persons covered: individuals, partnerships and companies? The position of hybrids.
2) The fixed base: retain the concept, merge with permanent establishment or re-define as, for example, a fixed place of activity?
3) Attribution: are Articles 7 and 14 identical in their provisions?
4) How far do difficulties with independent personal services derive from the nature of the activities and how far from the status of the taxpayer, e.g. as a partner in a partnership?

Appendix 2: Outline on Employees as a Permanent Establishment

To what extent do employees assigned to a subsidiary constitute a permanent establishment for the parent company? Background note by the OECD Secretariat[1]

Introduction

1. In this era of globalization of the world's economies and increase in cross-border trade and investment flows, it is more and more frequent to have employees seconded or otherwise transferred[2] for relatively short periods of time to foreign subsidiaries of multinational companies.

2. Such transfers raise tax treaty issues for both the employees and the companies involved. The purpose of this note is to explore these issues in order to identify practical problems which could be usefully discussed at the seminar.[3]

3. At the outset, it should be noted that, as recognized in paragraph 7 of Article 5, the mere existence of a parent/subsidiary relationship between two enterprises will not in itself be relevant in determining whether a permanent establishment exists in the circumstances contemplated in this note, so that the discussion therein would be equally applicable in the absence of such a relationship. Clearly, however, this note refers to circumstances, i.e. assignment of employees, which are more likely to occur in the context of a parent/subsidiary relationship[4] than between independent enterprises.

1. While this note has been prepared by a member of the OECD Secretariat, the opinions expressed therein are solely those of the author and should not be attributed in any way to the OECD or to its Member countries.
2. For the purposes of this note, the terms 'assigned' and 'transferred' should receive their broadest possible meaning so as to cover any arrangement where an employee of the parent goes to work in premises belonging to a subsidiary.
3. This note refers to the State where the head office or parent company is located as the sending State and the State where the employee is transferred as the host State. It is assumed throughout this note that both States are linked by a tax treaty identical, for all relevant purposes, to the OECD Model Tax Convention.
4. Or in the context of sister companies or other associated companies, since the situation of such companies should not be different from that of a parent and a subsidiary once paragraph 7 of Article 5 applies to confirm that control is not, in itself, a factor that makes a company a permanent establishment of the other.

Circumstances in which the parent company may be considered to have a permanent establishment in relation to the activities of the employee

4. The provisions of Article 5 of the Model Tax Convention may be said to consider two different types of permanent establishment: the 'fixed-place-of-business permanent establishment' and the 'agency permanent establishment'. Both types may be relevant in the case of employees assigned to work in a subsidiary's premises.

Fixed-place-of-business permanent establishment

5. Where a particular location is used by an employee of a parent company to perform activities, that particular location will constitute a fixed-place-of-business permanent establishment of the parent company, if, first, it constitutes a place of business through which the business of the parent company is wholly or partly carried on; second, there is a certain link between that place of business and a specific geographical point, and, third, that link has a certain degree of permanency.

6. In order to determine whether the first requirement is met, i.e. that the location is a place of business through which the activities of the parent company are carried on, it will thus be necessary to identify a business activity of the parent company that is carried on by the employee. Part of the business activities of the parent company may well be the management or supervision of its subsidiaries or the periodic assignment of temporary or expert workers world-wide so that an employee whose work on the subsidiary's premises would be related to these activities could therefore be said to be carrying on the business of the parent company. There may be cases, however, where the employee would be transferred to a subsidiary on an exceptional basis, for example, to help the subsidiary meet a temporary shortage of qualified workers, in circumstances where the employee will be performing activities that clearly belong exclusively to the business carried on by the subsidiary. In such a case it may be difficult to link the activities of the employee to a business carried on by the parent company, especially if such transfers are not customary; it would not seem enough merely to argue that the employee's activities reflect the interest of the parent company, as a shareholder, in the efficient operation of the subsidiary.

7. As regards the second and third requirements referred to in paragraph 5 above, it is well known that there is a certain degree of uncertainty in the practical application of both these geographical and time requirements.

8. The geographical requirement may well be satisfied where, for example, an office[5] is provided to the employee by the subsidiary, which will often be the case where the employee is doing management-type or consultancy work. Apart from the fact that an office would seem to come naturally under the meaning of 'fixed place of business', paragraph 2 of Article 5 of the Model Tax Convention specifically includes an 'office' in the list of examples that constitute *prima facie* a permanent establishment. Paragraph 4 of the Commentary on Article 5, and in particular the third sentence thereof, makes it clear that it is not relevant that the office provided by the subsidiary to an employee of the parent company is not owned nor rented by the parent company as it is 'otherwise at its disposal', i.e. at the disposal of its employee.

9. Where an employee of the parent company is involved in the management of a business operated by a subsidiary, one could ask, on a literal reading of the deeming provisions of paragraph 2 of Article 5, whether the place from which he will provide his activities could not also constitute a 'place of management' referred to in that paragraph. For instance, if a company, the business of which is to manage hotels, sends an employee to act as the temporary manager of an hotel owned and operated by one of its subsidiaries, does that constitute a 'place of management' referred to in paragraph 2 of Article 5 and, therefore, a permanent establishment of the parent company? Regardless of whether a permanent establishment would otherwise exist under paragraphs 1 or 2, the better interpretation, however, is that the 'place of management' referred to in paragraph 2 refers to a place for the management of the enterprise to which a permanent establishment is to be attributed, as opposed to a place from which other enterprises would be managed by that enterprise.

10. In practice, it may be difficult to determine when an office is actually at the disposal of the parent company.[6] Leaving aside the question of what constitutes

5. Note however that paragraph 4 of the Commentary on Article 5 indicates that a place of business could be constituted by something that would fall short of constituting an office: 'the term "place of business" covers any premises, facilities or installations used for carrying on the business of the enterprise whether or not they are used exclusively for that purpose. A place of business may also exist where no premises are available or required for carrying on the business of the enterprise and it simply has a certain amount of space at its disposal.'
6. In that respect, whether or not the parent company has a legally enforceable right to occupy the office would not seem to be relevant. The mere fact that the business of the parent is carried on in the office, regardless of whether the parent has the right to do so or that the presence of its employee therein is merely tolerated, should be enough to conclude that there is a permanent establishment, provided, of course, that this arrangement has a certain 'degree of permanency'.

an office, there may be cases where a number of different offices are available to both the employees of the subsidiary and the employee of the parent so that no particular office is assigned to any of these persons. There is, however, no requirement in Article 5 that a place of business be used exclusively by an enterprise in order to constitute a permanent establishment.[7] An office may therefore be a permanent establishment of a parent company even if part of the office is used at all times, or the whole office is used at certain times, for the business of the subsidiary.

11. With respect to the required 'degree of permanency', paragraph 6 of the Commentary indicates that a place of business should not be 'of a purely temporary nature'. The second sentence of that paragraph 5, however, stresses that the application of that test depends on the nature of that business; a business which is itself of limited duration could therefore have a permanent establishment that would exist for a limited time.

12. There is, of course, a large number of court decisions and rulings which have dealt with the issue of establishing a time threshold for the existence of a permanent establishment in particular circumstances. While these decisions and rulings are informative, it must be recognized that this is essentially an issue to be dealt with on a case-by-case basis. Given that business activities vary widely, it may not be possible to provide meaningful guidelines, such as a minimum time threshold. Nevertheless, this is an area where the views of IFA would be welcome.

Agency permanent establishment

13. Turning to the issue of the 'agency permanent establishment', the first question to be considered will be whether the employee, once assigned to the subsidiary, will constitute a person acting in the name of the parent company who will not be an independent agent to whom paragraph 6 of Article 5 is applicable.

14. While it is clear that an employee could hardly constitute an independent agent *vis-à-vis* his employer, the conditions under which the employee will be assigned to the subsidiary may be such that, notwithstanding the fact that he

7. As indicated in note 5, a place can be a 'place of business' used for carrying on the business of a foreign enterprise whether or not it is used exclusively for that purpose.

continues to be paid by the parent company, his employer may nonetheless be said to be the subsidiary. This will depend on the domestic law of each State and the factors listed in paragraph 8 of the Commentary on Article 15 could be relevant, regardless of the fact that the transfer arrangements may not have been tax-motivated. If the employee is, in fact, working for the subsidiary, he could hardly be said to be acting in the name of the parent company.

15. Assuming that the employee assigned to the subsidiary truly remains an employee of the parent company so that he is acting in the name of the parent company, it seems clear that he will not be an independent agent to whom paragraph 6 of Article 5 is applicable. Hence, the question of whether the parent company may be said to have an 'agency permanent establishment' boils down to whether the employee has, and habitually exercises, in the host State an authority to conclude contracts on behalf of that company.[8]

16. Where the activities of the employee in the host country are strictly technical, it is unlikely that this will be the case. It might be that the employee will keep the authority to conclude contracts that he had, and used, in the sending State; because the nature of his functions in the host State, however, will not require him from habitually exercising this right, the last condition for the 'agency permanent establishment' will not be met.

17. Where, however, the activities of the employee are of a managerial or consultative nature, the issue might be somewhat more difficult. It might be that, in managing or advising the subsidiary, the employee will himself decide to carry certain activities or undertake certain projects that would, between independent persons, require a contractual relationship.

18. Assume, for instance, that a senior accountant from the parent company is asked to review a subsidiary's accounting practices. Once in the host country where the subsidiary is located, he discovers that the practices followed by the subsidiary are deficient. After getting authorization from a supervisor in the parent company, he convinces ('informs' might be a better word, depending on the relationship between the subsidiary and the parent) the subsidiary's senior managers that he should stay on for a few months to implement appropriate changes to these practices and that, in accordance with the transfer pricing policy

8. It must be emphasized, in that respect, that paragraph 5 does not require a person to be a resident of the host State in order to constitute an agency permanent establishment therein.

of the parent company, a management fee equal to 115% of his salary plus fringe benefits will be charged by the parent company to the subsidiary for that work.

19. In such circumstances, it would appear that a contract, albeit a non-written one, has been concluded between the parent company and the subsidiary for the provision of services and that the employee had the authority to conclude that contract on behalf of the parent company, which he did.

20. As long, however, as only one such contract may be said to have been concluded by the employee, the condition, in paragraph 5, that the employee must 'habitually exercise' the authority to conclude the contract would not be satisfied. Suppose, however, that in carrying out changes to the accounting practices of the subsidiary, the employee will arrange for the subsidiary to acquire from the parent company various products (e.g. accounting software developed for, and used by, the parent company) and related services, so that he may be said to have concluded other contracts. It is, of course, impossible to say how many contracts need to be concluded in a given period of time to consider that the 'habitually exercise' condition is met. Paragraph 31 of the Commentary on Article 5 indicates that the authority to conclude contracts must be used 'repeatedly and not merely in isolated cases'. More likely than not, this can only be determined on the basis of all relevant facts, including the type of business involved.[9] One interesting issue, however, is whether the requirement to 'habitually exercise' an authority to conclude contracts may be satisfied if that authority is exercised frequently but during only a relatively short period of time.

21. Another aspect of the problem is the nature of the contracts concluded in such circumstances. Paragraph 33 indicates that the 'authority to conclude contracts must cover contracts relating to the operations which constitute the business proper of the enterprise'. The paragraph then goes on, however, to clarify that this is intended to distinguish the case of a person who has the authority to conclude business contracts from the person who has merely the authority to conclude contracts related to internal operations, such as the hiring of an assistant. In the example given above, it would seem that since the contract is directly

9. In the United States, two of the 'race-horse' rulings (a 1981 private letter ruling – letter ruling 8138020 – and Revenue ruling 85–4–1985–2 C.B. 6) could be read to suggest that two contracts would be sufficient in some circumstances. On the other hand, in *Alphawell*, a decision of the Norwegian Supreme Court, the conclusion of a contract between a company owned by a geologist and an oil company, which was followed by three or four renewals of that contract, was found not to meet the 'habitually exercise' test.

income-generating, the type of contract would fall in the first rather than in the second category and would therefore be of the kind contemplated by paragraph 5.

22. A practical difficulty that would confront any attempt to find an agency permanent establishment in the context of an employee of a parent company temporarily transferred to a subsidiary is the fact that, while the employee may make decisions or suggestions that would lead to formal contracts if he were representing an independent enterprise, the nature of the parent-subsidiary relationship will make it such that the contractual relationship may not be well documented. In the example above, if the employee had represented an independent enterprise, he might have concluded different contracts (e.g. services of improving accounting procedures and sale of the accounting software). Where, however, the parent company's employee has received a broad mandate from its employer that results in various types of services being acquired by the subsidiary from the parent, there may not be much more than a single end-of-year charge from the parent to the subsidiary to cover the various transactions. While transfer pricing rules might assume various contracts in these circumstances, it is not clear to what extent these contracts would exist for purposes of determining whether an agency permanent establishment would exist under paragraph 5.

Preparatory or auxiliary activities

23. The nature of the activities performed by the employee for the parent company may also be relevant in determining whether the circumstances of his assignment to the subsidiary are such that a permanent establishment of the parent company may be said to exist: if these activities fall within the categories included in paragraph 4 of Article 5, no permanent establishment will exist. Thus, where an employee of the parent company regularly uses an office in premises owned by the subsidiary for the purposes of obtaining information for the parent company on the activities of the subsidiary, no permanent establishment would be said to exist.

Tax consequences resulting from a finding that there is a permanent establishment

24. To a large extent, where the circumstances of the assignment of a parent company's employee to a subsidiary are such that a permanent establishment of the parent company may be said to exist in the host country, the consequences may be more important for the employee than for the company.

25. The finding of a permanent establishment may have significant consequences for the parent company when the employee is engaged in transactions with third parties, such as activities leading to sales. For example, where the subsidiary regularly puts an office at the disposal of an employee of the parent company to discuss with potential customers, but in circumstances where the employee does not have the authority to conclude contracts, the office may constitute a permanent establishment of the parent company and the issue will be what part of the income from the sales resulting from the employee's activities should be attributed to that permanent establishment.

26. Where, however, the employee is engaged in providing services to the subsidiary, the impact on the parent company may be minimal. Indeed, where a permanent establishment exists in such circumstances, it will often be the case that the only income that may properly be attributable to the permanent establishment will be an arm's length charge for the services provided by the employee. Since the remuneration of the employee for the period during which the services are rendered will then be properly allowable as a deduction in computing such income, that will only leave the arm's length profit margin applicable to these services[10] as a taxable income of the parent company in the host country.

27. For the employee, however, the situation is different. The finding of a permanent establishment of the parent company may well mean the difference between becoming subject to taxation in the host country or remaining taxable only in the sending State.[11]

28. Let us assume that the employee remains resident of the sending State, this status resulting from either the domestic laws of the host State or the application of the tie-breaker rules[12] of the relevant tax treaty.[13] Since the employment, during the period of transfer, will be exercised in the host State, that State will

10. This assumes, of course, that the circumstances in which the services are rendered are such that it may be considered that services are effectively provided by the parent company to the subsidiary (*cf.* OECD Guidelines on Transfer Pricing).
11. It may be, however, that the parent company will agree to bear any tax cost, for the employee, resulting from his assignment abroad. In that case, the finding of a permanent establishment will obviously have a greater impact on the employer.
12. Paragraph 2 of Article 4 of the OECD Model Tax Convention.
13. While in both cases the employee would not be a resident of the host State for purposes of the application of the tax treaty, it is acknowledged that the two cases may trigger different tax consequences in the application of the domestic tax laws of the host State; this difference in treatment, however, will not be discussed in this note which focuses exclusively on treaty issues.

have, under paragraph 1 of Article 15 of the tax treaty between the two States, the right to tax the remuneration therefrom unless the conditions of paragraph 2 of the same article are met. Assuming that the conditions of subparagraphs 2(a) and (b) are met so that the employee is not present in the host State for more than the maximum period referred to in subparagraph (a) and that his employer is not a resident of the host State,[14] the issue will be whether the condition of subparagraph (c), which reads as follows, is met:

> '(c) the remuneration is not borne by a permanent establishment or a fixed base which the employer has in the other State.'

29. The condition of subparagraph (c) will not be met if it can be established that the presence of the employee constitutes a permanent establishment of the parent company. If that is the case, the employee's remuneration would almost certainly be taxable in the host country as it does not seem possible to imagine a case where the remuneration would not be borne by the permanent establishment (paragraph 3 of Article 7 would require the remuneration of the employee to be allowed as deduction in computing the profits attributable to the permanent establishment).

30. The fact that the employee is likely to be more affected than the parent company does not mean, however, that the issue of whether a permanent establishment exists has little practical importance. There are cases where the remuneration of the employee may represent a relatively large amount. For example, there are cases where the president of the subsidiary, who is also the sole shareholder of the parent company, manages the subsidiary from the sending State but make frequent visits to the subsidiary's offices. There are also cases where many of the subsidiary high-level managers are provided by the parent company on a rotating basis.

14. Subparagraph (b) requires that 'the remuneration is paid by, or an behalf of, an employer who is not a resident of the other State [the host State]'. The arrangements between the parent company and the subsidiary and the domestic law of the host State will be relevant in determining whether that condition is met. As already noted (*see* paragraph 14 above), there may well be cases where, even if the employee is formally paid by the parent company, the employer may be said to be the subsidiary as the employee comes under the direct supervision and control of managers of the subsidiary (the factors listed in paragraph 8 of the Commentary on Article 15 may be relevant in that respect) and the subsidiary reimburses the salary of the employee to the parent so that this remuneration may be said to be paid 'on behalf of' the subsidiary.

APPENDIX 2: OUTLINE ON EMPLOYEES AS A PERMANENT ESTABLISHMENT

Overhead No. 1

EMPLOYEE IS ASSIGNED TO A SUBSIDIARY SO AS TO WORK IN PREMISES BELONGING TO THE SUBSIDIARY (E.G. THE EMPLOYEE USES AN OFFICE PROVIDED BY THE SUBSIDIARY)

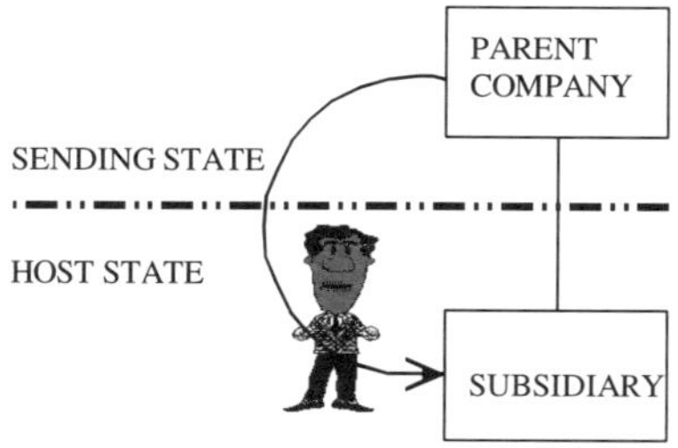

Overhead No. 2

FIXED-PLACE-OF-BUSINESS PERMANENT ESTABLISHMENT

- A LOCATION USED BY THE EMPLOYEE IN THE HOST STATE
- THE LOCATION IS A PLACE OF BUSINESS THROUGH WHICH A BUSINESS OF THE PARENT COMPANY IS WHOLLY OR PARTLY CARRIED ON
- THERE IS A CERTAIN LINK BETWEEN THAT PLACE OF BUSINESS AND A SPECIFIC GEOGRAPHICAL POINT
- THE PLACE OF BUSINESS HAS A CERTAIN DEGREE OF PERMANENCY

Overhead No. 3

AGENCY PERMANENT ESTABLISHMENT

- THE EMPLOYEE CONSTITUTES A PERSON ACTING IN THE NAME OF THE PARENT COMPANY
- THE EMPLOYEE HAS THE AUTHORITY TO CONCLUDE CONTRACTS ON BEHALF OF THE PARENT COMPANY
- THE EMPLOYEE HABITUALLY EXERCISES THAT AUTHORITY

Overhead No. 4

SENIOR ACCOUNTANT SENT TO REVIEW THE ACCOUNTING PRACTICES OF THE SUBSIDIARY
MOVES FROM OFFICE TO OFFICE IN THE SUBSIDIARY HEADQUARTERS
HE DECIDES TO IMPLEMENT CHANGES IN THE ACCOUNTING PRACTICES
HE ARRANGES FOR THE SUBSIDIARY TO ACQUIRE VARIOUS PRODUCTS AND SERVICES FROM THE PARENT COMPANY (E.G. SOFTWARE ETC.)
A MANAGEMENT FEE EQUAL TO 115% OF HIS SALARY WILL BE CHARGED TO THE SUBSIDIARY

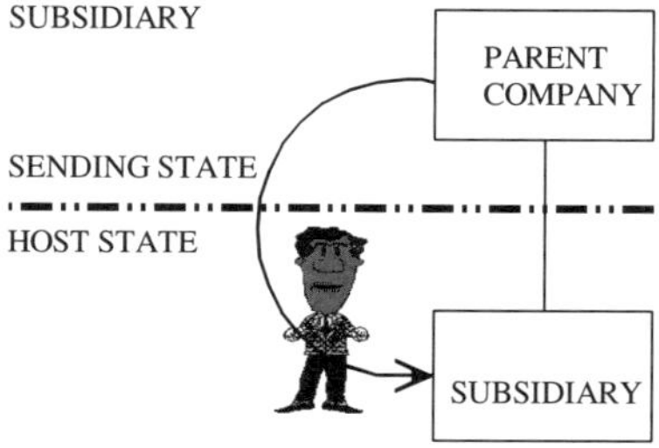

Overhead No. 5

FIXED-PLACE-OF-BUSINESS PERMANENT ESTABLISHMENT

- WHAT IS THE BUSINESS OF THE PARENT COMPANY THAT IS CARRIED ON IN THE OFFICES?
- CAN A NUMBER OF OFFICES USED BY THE EMPLOYEE IN THE SAME BUILDING CONSTITUTE ONE PLACE OF BUSINESS (I.E. IS THE LINK WITH A SPECIFIC GEOGRAPHICAL POINT SUFFICIENT)?
- SHOULD THE PARENT COMPANY HAVE A LEGALLY ENFORCEABLE RIGHT TO USE THE OFFICES?
- HOW LONG SHOULD THE EMPLOYEE USE THE OFFICES FOR THEM TO CONSTITUTE A PERMANENT ESTABLISHMENT?

Overhead No. 6

AGENCY PERMANENT ESTABLISHMENT

- IS THE ACCOUNTANT ACTING IN THE NAME OF THE PARENT COMPANY?
- DOES HE HAVE AN AUTHORITY TO CONCLUDE CONTRACTS?
- ARE THESE CONTRACTS RELATED TO A BUSINESS OF THE PARENT COMPANY?
- IS THE AUTHORITY TO CONCLUDE CONTRACTS "HABITUALLY EXERCISED"?

Overhead No. 7

IF THE COMPANY HAS A PERMANENT ESTABLISHMENT

- WHAT INCOME IS TAXABLE IN THE HOST STATE?
- WHAT ARE THE TAX CONSEQUENCES FOR THE EMPLOYEE?

Appendix 3: The Origins of OECD Model Articles 7, 14 and 15[1]

Mexico (1943) and London (1946) Model Tax Conventions

1. Article IV of the Mexico draft dealt with 'income from any industrial, commercial or agricultural business and from any other gainful activity'. The Commentary approved the use of the term 'business profits' for such income.

2. The profits were to be taxable only in the State where the business or activity was carried out. If an enterprise or an individual in one of the States extended its or his activities to the other State through isolated or occasional transactions, without possessing in that State a permanent establishment, the income derived from such activities was to be taxable only in the residence State.

3. If the enterprise had a permanent establishment in both States, each State was to tax that part of the income which was produced in its territory. There is no express equivalent of this provision for individuals. However, the Protocol to the Mexico draft said that the term 'enterprise' included any kind of enterprise whether it belonged to an individual, a partnership, a company or any other legal entity or *de facto* body. So presumably it was intended that this rule would apply whether the enterprise belonged to an individual or to a company.

4. Article IV of the London draft is similar. It refers to 'income derived from ... any other gainful *occupation*' (rather than 'gainful activity'), although the Commentary does not make anything of this difference and it is clear that 'occupation' was not used in the sense of 'employment'. The London draft refers simply to 'enterprise', and not to 'individual'; and makes more determined use of the criterion of permanent establishment for allocating taxing rights.

5. The Protocol to the London draft contains the same definition of the term 'enterprise' as the Protocol to the Mexico draft. The Protocols to both drafts contain provisions concerning the allocation of the income of enterprises mentioned in Article IV 'in respect of industrial, commercial and agricultural enterprises in general and for other independent activities'. It appears that the

1. An informal note prepared for OECD Working Party No. 1 purposes by Mr. M. Waters.

last phrase is simply intended as an alternative for 'other gainful activity/occupation' which is the term used in Article IV. As mentioned below, the Mexico and the London drafts contain separate rules for income from professions. There does not appear to be any connection between the use of 'other independent activities' in connection with Article IV of the Mexico and London drafts and the use of 'activities of an independent character' and 'independent activities' in the modern OECD Model Article 14.

6. Article VII of the Mexico draft and Article VI of the London draft dealt with income 'for labour or personal services'. The Commentary uses in connection with these Articles the phrase 'remuneration from personal services and private employment' and goes on to say that they are intended to cover earnings from all private employments and professions.

7. Both Articles contained forerunners of the modern 183–day rule but applying to private employments and to professions alike.

8. The Articles also contained provisions which the Commentary noted dealt specifically with independent professions and embodied rules similar to those in Article IV relating taxation of income to the existence of a permanent establishment, a term which was not confined to Article IV. The Protocols to the Mexico and the London drafts discuss the term 'permanent establishment' and include 'professional premises' among the examples. Articles VII/VI referred to income derived by an accountant, an architect, a doctor or physician, an engineer and a lawyer or 'other person engaged in the practice of a liberal profession' (Mexico) / 'other person engaged on his own account in the practice of a profession' (London). The Commentary makes nothing of these differences in wording which were not, therefore, presumably intended to convey a different meaning.

9. One might conclude from the above that:

a. Article IV of the Mexico and London drafts is the clear forerunner of OECD Model Article 7. Thus the former refers to 'income from any industrial, commercial ... business'; and it is clearly implied in paragraphs 1 and 4 of the Commentary on OECD Model Article 14 that Article 7 of the Model deals with profits from industrial and commercial activities. This is reflected also in paragraph 35 of the Commentary on Article 7. Moreover, income and profits which are within the Mexico and London Articles may be derived by companies or by individuals.

b. The Mexico and London drafts dealt in a single Article with what we would now regard as income from independent personal services on the one hand and income from dependent personal services on the other. By covering both types of income in the same Article, the Mexico and London drafts seem to have assumed that they were derived by individuals but could not be derived by companies. This was underlined by the reference to 'personal services' in the Articles; and is perhaps underlined more in the London draft by the use of the phrase 'other person engaged *on his own account* in the practice of a profession'.

The work of the OEEC and the OECD

10. Between 1958 and 1961 the Fiscal Committee of the Organization for European Economic Co-operation (OEEC) published four reports which built on the work of the Mexico and London drafts and led directly to the first Model Convention published by the OECD in 1963.

11. In September 1958 the OEEC published an Article dealing with permanent establishments. The examples no longer included 'professional premises' (contrast paragraph 8 above). In a Commentary the OEEC noted that the term 'professional premises' might in some instances be covered by the more general term 'office'.

12. In its second report published in July 1959 the OEEC produced a number of Articles which collectively were said to deal with the taxation of income in respect of independent and dependent personal services. They were the forerunners of OECD Model Articles 14–20. In particular, OEEC Article VI is virtually identical to OECD Model Article 14(1). One of the differences is that Article VI refers to 'professional services or other independent activities of a similar character'. This form of words was taken into the OECD Model in 1963 but was amended in 1977 to the current version 'professional services or other activities of an independent character'. (Paragraph (2) of Model Article 14 was added by the OECD in 1963.)

13. So the OEEC seems to have been the first international organization which, in 1959, recommended putting income from professional/independent personal services and income from dependent personal services into separate Articles and the use of the term 'fixed base regularly available' in connection with the former.

14. In making both these changes the OEEC said that it was following the example of various States which were already concluding conventions along those lines. In particular it noted that the term 'fixed base' was already to be found in various conventions. An early use of the concept (if not of the term 'fixed base' in its modern form) is found in the France/Sweden treaty of 1936. This provided that taxes on earned income, including from professional services, were to be levied only in the State in which the personal activities giving rise to the income were exercised. Professional services were to be regarded as rendered in a State only if '*l'activité professionnelle a un point d'attache fixe*' in that State (the modern French term for 'fixed base' is '*base fixe*').

15. In the case of the UK, it had been customary to include professional services and employments in a single Article dealing with 'personal (including professional) services' without any reference to a concept similar to permanent establishment or fixed base. This policy gradually changed. Under the 1951 UK/France treaty an individual who was a resident of one State was to be exempt from tax in the other State on employment income from services performed in the other State if he had no 'office or other fixed place of business' in the other State. The same test appeared in the 1954 UK/Belgium treaty concerning taxation of income from carrying on a profession. Then under the 1955 UK/Germany treaty profits from a profession exercised in one State by a resident of the other State were to be taxable in the first State only if the individual had a fixed base in the first State from which to carry on his professional activity. The 1957 UK/Austria treaty used 'fixed accommodation which is regularly at [the individual's] disposal'.

16. The OEEC Commentary on Article VI is virtually identical to paragraphs 1 and 4 of the Commentary on OECD Model Article 14. (Paragraph 2 of the OECD Commentary was added in 1963; and paragraph 3 was added in 1977 and was amended in 1992 by the addition of the closing couple of lines.)

17. Also in 1959 the OEEC included references to fixed bases in the forerunners of OECD Model Articles 15 and 22.

18. In its fourth report, published in August 1961, the OEEC published Articles on the taxation of dividends, interest and royalties. These Articles contained the forerunners of OECD Model Articles 10(4), 11(4), 11(5) and 12(3). These all referred to permanent establishments but not to fixed bases. No explanation was given for the absence of references to fixed bases. (As regards the other Articles which refer to fixed bases, the OEEC did not publish an Article dealing with

capital gains; and paragraph (2) of Model Article 21 was not added by the OECD until 1977.)

19. It is possible that the absence of a reference to fixed bases in OECD Model Article 24(3) is attributable to the fact that that provision clearly derives from the equivalent Article published by the OEEC in its first report in 1958, a year before it published the Article dealing with independent personal services which used the term 'fixed base' for the first time. However, that would not explain the absence of references to fixed bases in the forerunners of Articles 10–12 which were published by the OEEC two years after the Article on independent personal services. OECD also did not include references to fixed bases in Articles 10–12 in the Model which it published in 1963: they were not added until 1977. The Commentary on Model Article 11(5) still does not refer to fixed bases, except in the alternative version of the provision quoted in paragraph 30 of the Commentary.